THE INNER RING

THE OLIVER PUBLISHING GROUP, INC.

First printing April 1995
Second printing August 1995

Printed in the United States of America
Printed by: Hallmark Press, Inc., Miami, Florida
Art Director / Cover Design: Frank Oliver
Illustrations: Nicholas Nathaniel
Published by: The Oliver Publishing Group, Inc.
ISBN 0-9646644-0-2

ATTENTION ORGANIZATIONS: Quantity discounts are available on bulk purchases of this book for educational purposes or fund raising. Special books or book excerpts can also be created to fit specific needs. For information, please contact:

The Oliver Publishing Group, Inc.
100 S.E. 2nd Street
Suite 2750
Miami, Florida 33131-2146
Phone: (305) 372-0946 / Fax (305) 372-0947.

PREFACE

One day in late January of this year, I ran into an old acquaintance, Martha Lopez, on the third floor of the Metro Justice Building where I had just attended a hearing in a criminal case. Martha and I had worked together years before in the old U.S. Justice Department Building at 155 South Miami Avenue in downtown Miami. It had been almost three years since we had last seen each other. Martha mentioned that she recently had received a license in the bail bonding business. I told her I'd give her a call if one of my clients ever needed to bond out of jail.

Several weeks later, Martha called me about something completely unrelated to her new career. As I understood it, her boyfriend was interested in telling the story about his experiences working for a celebrity. "I remembered how you love to write," she said. Although I didn't recall ever showing her anything I had done, she was right. Writers who can spin out a touching story, who can "move" the reader, always have been special heros for me. I once authored an article published in the University of Miami Law Review entitled "Can Retreads Be As Good As New?" It dealt with my experiences pursuing the study of law at night school as a second career while in my mid-thirties. One of the themes was how grateful I was to family and friends for their support and sacrifice during that long and difficult process. Sometime after it was published, a young lady called me out of the blue:

i

"Mr. Feigenbaum, I had tears in my eyes when I finished your article." I knew from that moment forward that this was what I most liked to do, tell a story which, if I were lucky, would "move" somebody. I still had no idea what this all was about, but told Martha to swing by the house around 8 p.m. with her boyfriend.

When the doorbell rang, Martha was standing there with a young man who reminded me of Erik Estrada from the old "C.H.I.P.S." series. He was wearing an expensive-looking leather jacket with the inscription "Team Tyson." That night I sat with Martha and my wife and listened to Rudy Gonzalez relate certain events of the past eight years, most of which he spent working as chauffeur, personal aide, and bodyguard to former world-heavyweight boxing champion Mike Tyson. For the next five hours I sat spellbound. His story fascinated me. It was about a servant, stubbornly loyal, who still believed that he worked for Mike Tyson, even though he hadn't been paid in more than three years. And, although he no longer was chauffeuring around and protecting "MT," who had been sitting alone in a cold prison cell in Plainfield, Indiana, since early 1992, Rudy's "job" as he saw it was to do everything he could to tell this story to a world which, if he were lucky, would be interested in knowing the truth. And, if he were lucky, this story also just might protect Mike Tyson, and perhaps others, from the the type of deceit, and betrayal, and fraud committed upon him in the past.

Although Rudy and Martha had to leave, I wanted to hear more. "I'll tell you more if you agree to write this story," he said. "Why me?" I asked. Martha's answer was simple: "I told Rudy you write with passion." It didn't take me long to decide. "But you have to write it in two weeks," Rudy added. "Mike Tyson is scheduled to be released by the end of March. I want him to have this story when he leaves prison." Rudy was very tired from everything that had been happening to him over the past few years. There had been too many empty promises. "Two weeks?" I made some quick calculations. "Okay, but two weeks from the time you give me the last information that needs to go into the story." On a handshake, we began the process which resulted in this book.

There are several people who deserve a great deal of credit for assisting in this project. Martha Lopez helped out enormously by collecting and assembling a great deal of the materials contained in this book. My legal assistant, Tricia Menendez, did fact-checking, making innumerable calls all over the country. My son Lou, a fine athlete, general sports enthusiast, and Mike Tyson fan, spent many hours at the University of Miami library researching and documenting certain events. And finally, Frank Oliver, one of the most creative people I've met and a graphic art genius, contributed hundreds of hours to every facet of this project.

Miami, March 3, 1995

*In Memory of Cus D'Amato
and
all fighters everywhere, who have given
their wealth, freedom, and even their lives
to the sport of professional boxing.*

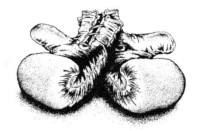

Dedication

To my Mother, Elizabeth, thanks for giving me life, hopes, and dreams.

To my Father, big Rudy, for keeping the world off my shoulders.

To my Sister, Evelyn, for just being a sister.

To Martha L. Gonzalez, my companion, my inspiration, my friend and *my wife*. I Love You.

To the memory of The Honorable Robert Rodriguez, a man who was like an uncle to me. He taught me respect, honesty, and loyalty. I will never ever forget you.

To Alfonso "Grandpa" Miranda, "let's get to the point." You made it all happen.

To Frank Oliver, I couldn't have completed this project without your mind meld.

To Arthur Corbière, for being you, and for being here for me.

To Marty Feigenbaum, thank you for being a heavyweight champion of words.

and,

To Mike Tyson, *I miss you.*

RUDY GONZALEZ
April 1995

This is a book that only could have been written by someone who loved Mike Tyson and was his devoted man Friday as well as his personal chauffeur.

Rudy Gonzalez was not only at Mike's service and present at all times, as it turned out he was more! He was the "fly on the wall" so to speak.

Here Rudy reveals some of the most sad and shocking stories behind the headlines and behind the facades. An incredible story told by Rudy Gonzalez with the superb collaboration of Martin Feigenbaum.

Bill Cayton

Bill Cayton, former Tyson manager from the original "Team Tyson"

"YO!"

"The Jacket"

"Gotta' Have It Givens"

"Bait & Switch"

"The Kingdom of Darkness"

"From the Darkness Comes a Whisper"

"Just Sign Here"

"Final Errands"

"The Final Round"

"YO!"

The first year I chauffeured Mike Tyson around, he didn't know my name. He just called me "Yo!" I was working full-time during the day for United Parcel Service and part-time at night driving for Michelle's limousine service. Around 3:00 a.m. one very cold November morning in 1986, someone placed a credit-card order to pick up an unknown party at Kennedy Airport. I was told the party would recognize the limousine. The dispatcher called me because the job was too much of a dog for one of the regular drivers. Although I had been on Michelle's list of available part-timers for more than three months, this was to be my first call. A few days earlier, on November 22, Mike Tyson captivated the world by capturing the WBC heavyweight title, knocking out Trevor Berbick in the second round at the Las Vegas Hilton. At age 20, this made Mike Tyson the youngest world-heavyweight champion in history. Had the dispatcher known that the party waiting at JFK was the famous newly-crowned champion, she never would have assigned me that job.

In early 1992 Mike Tyson was convicted and sentenced for raping an eighteen-year-old Miss Black America beauty contestant, Desiree Washington, on July 19, 1991. By that time, more than anyone else, I knew what really had been going on in Tyson's life. By that time, I had heard and seen too much because I had been with Tyson around the clock the past five years. By that time, I was the most dangerous man in the boxing world, even though I wasn't a professional fighter. I knew about the deception and fraud that had befallen Mike

1

Tyson. A few days after we discovered it together, sitting on the floor of his bedroom in Las Vegas, I was the victim of an assassination attempt while running an errand in Los Angeles.

Mike Tyson disappeared behind the walls of a prison in Plainfield wearing number 922335, a prisoner of the State of Indiana. I know now that, instead, he should have been wearing the heavyweight champion belt as a free man. I know that now because I have the proof.

I signed on as a part-time limousine driver for Michelle's because I was looking for excitement. The owner of the company, Ruth Goldberg, had known me from my days at the Playboy Club in Manhattan's Lexington Hotel. One evening, I was home watching *Entertainment Tonight*, and there was a piece on a new direction the Playboy Clubs were taking. To get in tune with the eighties and attract a female clientele, the Hefner organization had decided there also should be "rabbits" as well as "bunnies." The next morning I was on the phone with Playboy Enterprises, located at Third Avenue and 56th Street, trying to get information about the auditions. Three days later I showed up with a photo and bathing suit and stood for hours outside the building in a long line. Every type of actor and model was there, and I was convinced I didn't stand a chance to get hired. Eventually I ended up inside, feeling embarrassed and foolish parading around in only my trunks. I noticed that almost everybody was being sent away with a simple thank you, but somehow I made it to the next stage, instructed to go upstairs and fill out an application. For two weeks I waited around and then finally got a call. The Playboy Club wanted a second "audition" in which they took some photos, asked a lot of questions, and again said they'd let me know. Several weeks passed before I learned I was a "finalist." They called me in for a meeting and told me they were hiring representatives of different nationalities and races. I fit the Hispanic profile. Later I learned that I was a "first runner up," not good enough to be hired for opening night three weeks away, but they would call me if anything changed.

When I got home from work on the day the rabbits were going to make their much publicized debut, there was a message on my answering machine. One of the original rabbits had been arrested, and they wanted to know if I could run down to the Club right away and report for a costume fitting. They already had given me some training so I was ready for my assignment as a backup bartender at one of the service bars. After a few days I was promoted to running the service bar, and not long after that moved up to the huge Octagon bar which sold an average of 800 drinks a night. At the service bar I had been taking home around $100, but at the Octagon my earnings soared to between $300 to $500 a night. I was twenty-four years old. That's how I met Ruth Goldberg who along with her husband owned Michelle's limousine service. She came often to the Club alone, always asking for "Rudy the Rabbit," ordering one glass of wine, and leaving me a $100 tip each time.

During the two years I worked there, the Playboy Club appeared to be a big success, attracting a strange mix of celebrities, Elizabeth Taylor, Dr. Ruth Westheimer, Sylvester Stallone, Malcolm Forbes, Howard Stern, Montel Williams, Gregory Hines. Mike Tyson was even there once in 1985, accompanied by Freddie Jackson and rappers LL Cool Jay and Run-D.M.C., but I didn't meet my future boss that night. My Club days provided me money and sex far beyond my wildest dreams. There always were women waiting around until closing time to see if they could take a rabbit home to bed. And the bunnies preferred to date us because they trusted

4

us as fellow employees. It was very much a fantasy existence while it lasted.

One day very much to my surprise, Christy Hefner announced that a business decision had been made to shut the doors of the entire chain of Playboy Clubs. It sure seemed to me like the Clubs were big moneymakers. I was going to sorely miss this incredible lifestyle as well as the very professional Playboy management, people like Gerry Nobile who worked hard to ensure good employee relations. Anyway, as a consolation to Club employees, the organization flew all of us to Los Angeles, put us up in a hotel for several days, and invited us to the Playboy mansion for a big farewell bash. After that, it looked like my crazy and profitable days as "Rudy the Rabbit" were over. Over the years I have maintained contact with Gerry and others at Playboy who have remained good and loyal friends.

I had a lot of money saved up by then so I decided to take off for Rio de Janeiro. I stayed at the Copacabana for two months during which time I saw the famous Carnaval. After Brazil, I headed to Puerto Rico for awhile, met a girl, and brought her back to New York for a few weeks. I hung out doing mostly nothing for a good part of 1986, desperately avoiding having to deal with my future. I used some of my savings to fix up my Mom's building located in the middle of Spanish Harlem. She had lived there for as long as I could remember, most of the time without benefit of electricity or running water. Junkies kept stealing the copper wiring and water pipes to get money to feed their heroin habits. The landlord abandoned the building which was good only because we didn't have to pay rent. We lived as squatters with three other families for ten years before the City condemned it and took it over. As a child, I remember my Mother walking down five flights to get water, returning with a full pail and an aching back, so we could wash and cook. Sometimes we got electricity by hooking up an extension cord to a nearby utility pole.

Elizabeth didn't have anybody to help her out when I was growing up. My father, Rudolph, was in prison during most of my childhood. He was born of a mixed marriage, his father Italian, his mother from Barcelona, Spain. When my Father met my mother, who is Puerto Rican, his parents disapproved of this relationship, knowing that there were too many problems with "mixed" marriages. When my Father and Mother married, all ties were broken with his family. Before we were old enough to understand my Father was a career criminal, instead of a military man, she took us to visit him in prison. Mom told us he was working on an army project in a big building, constructing a robot for the government. There was a five-year period when I didn't see my Father at all. The little time he was around, I remember him mostly hanging out with fat guys smoking cigars on the streets of our neighborhood at 116th Street between First and Pleasant Avenues. Finally, Rudolph Gonzalez was convicted of drug trafficking, heroin and cocaine, and did eleven years in Sing Sing.

One of the guys from my neighborhood was Hector Camacho who later became the boxing champion "Macho"

6

Camacho. As a young kid, Hector took a lot of shit from his compadres for being such a "pretty boy." That's why he took up boxing, developing a "bad ass" reputation so anybody who teased him would get his ass kicked. Years later, incredible circumstances would make our paths cross once again in the world of professional boxing, and there would be both intrigue and betrayal. Pleasant Avenue was the unofficial border between the Italian and Puerto Rican neighborhoods. I could cross the Pleasant Avenue border with impunity because I had blood and friends from both sides. I also had a bad streak, and had proved it enough times, which gave me certain respect in the streets. But I also got along well with anybody unless and until they violated my trust. It was probably because I was this way that I survived longer than anybody else at Mike Tyson's side as he rose to acquire enormous fame, fortune, and power. But even though I was popular and accepted by both sides of Pleasant Avenue, Elizabeth still feared my being in the streets where getting shot was a daily occurrence. She would do anything to get me out of Spanish Harlem. So when I was twelve, she pleaded with my wealthy godmother, Carmen, to see if she would take me in at least for one summer at the Pizzollas' ranch estate in Rockland County.

Carmen and her older husband, Michael, owned a very profitable pizzeria and bakery in Manhattan, and they lived in a big house an hour north of the City, commuting to their business in their big Mercedes. That first summer away from Spanish Harlem, Carmen tried to turn me into a young "country gentleman," constantly showing me that there was

7

a "life beyond the streets." It was a world I had never known existed. We went to museums and art galleries, and she took me shopping so I would look like one of the rich kids from her part of the world. She also spoke to me a lot about how a man should treat a woman, how to keep her happy and in love with him. She also told me I would do great things and travel all over the world. Instead of returning home at the end of the summer, I stayed with the Pizzollas and went to school in Rockland County. My mother was convinced that I should stay with them, if they would have me, because it was better to be far away from her and safe, than near her and in danger in the streets below.

I did two years of junior high in Rockland County and summer camp at Valley Forge Military. When I was sixteen, things got crazy for the Pizzollas. There was a lot of news about heroin busts around the City. Drugs were being distributed through a network of pizzerias. An investigation of the Pizzollas was underway, and I detected the fear and tension in Carmen's life. She sent me back to live with my Mom, and shortly afterwards Carmen and Michael Pizzolla were indicted, convicted, and sent to jail. So by my sophomore year, I was back in my old neighborhood at 116th Street between First and Pleasant Avenues.

My high school, Julia Richmond, at 2nd Avenue between 65th and 68th Streets was a rough place. One summer it looked like they were doing major remodeling of the school library. When we returned in the fall, we realized a police annex had been built right inside the school, holding cells and all, and the library had been eliminated. The idea was to reduce police response time to make arrests. Back home permanently now from my life as a young "country gentlemen," and hanging out on the streets with a bad crowd, it didn't take long before I was arrested and locked up. A bunch of us had slipped into a drugstore looking to shoplift and resell cosmetics. Two of my partners in crime had guns so our shoplifting expedition became an armed robbery. We all were caught and charged. As a first-time offender, I plea-bargained my way to a fourteen month stay at Rikers detention center.

The only bright moment after my release was walking by a French restaurant, Chez Manoun, and catching sight of an incredibly beautiful girl holding menus. I started walking four blocks out of my way each day on the way home from school just to see the face of this hostess. I fell in love with her from a distance and wanted to work there. When one afternoon I saw a sign for a dishwasher job, I rushed inside and was greeted by her.

"Aren't you the guy who walks by here every day and stares at me?"

She smiled and helped me get the job. Her name was Melissa, and she was French-Canadian. Hanging around the chef, I learned to cook French food. When the chef didn't show up one night, left with no other choice, the owner gave me a chance to prove myself. Everything went so well he hired me as his regular chef. I kept the job even after I graduated, but after awhile I got bored with the daily routine.

Years later, I used this skill to occasionally cook for my boss, Mike Tyson. Because I was looking for something exciting to do, I considered bartending. That's when I caught the television piece about the Playboy "rabbits."

Now it was mid-1986, and I was still dwelling on the fact that, but for Carmen Pizzola's legal problems, I probably would have graduated from military school and gone onto college. But I had to face reality. My savings were gone from the extended trips to Brazil and Puerto Rico, fixing up my Mom's building, and goofing off for too long. I landed a job at United Parcel Service as a part-timer loading trucks. After a time, I began working a full shift, in the building three days supervising loading and unloading trucks, two days on the outside making deliveries. When I was delivering packages in Manhattan's fashion district, I saw many beautiful women, receptionists and models. Most didn't give me the time of day. It was a painful reminder of my fantasy life at the Playboy Club. I also kept thinking about what Carmen Pizzolla kept telling me when I lived at her ranch estate in Rockland County.

"Rudy, you're going to travel to many exotic places and meet beautiful people."

I don't think my life at this point in time was what she had in mind.

I was getting desperate to find something that could plug me into some excitement. With all the stories I had heard, I became obsessed with the idea of becoming a limousine driver. I remembered Ruth Goldberg, the lady who used to sit at the Octagon bar, drink one glass of wine, and leave me a $100 tip. Her limousine service had big-name clientele because it had Rolls Royces available. This was the kind of prestigious company I believed would provide me the excitement I was craving. So one day I went by her place of business. She was delighted to see me, said she could use me, and had me fill out an application. Three months went by without a call while I continued my daily routine at UPS.

Around 3:00 a.m. on November 29, the phone rang. My Mother answered and called out that there was a lady asking for me. Before she handed me the phone, she wanted to know what the hell I was doing taking on a job with a limousine service where I would be out all night and lose my job at UPS. I told her I was looking for some excitement, not to worry, that I could do both.

"This is the dispatcher. Your name was on the standby driver list. Get your butt down to the garage. We've got a pick-up at JFK."

Winter 1986 was very harsh. There was a lot of snow on the ground, and the cold air blasted me in the face as I tried to flag down a private cab. You can't find a Yellow Cab at 3:00 a.m. in Spanish Harlem no matter what time of year. I was getting nervous because I had to get to 125th and

Riverside Drive in the next few minutes, or I would be fired for sure, without ever having driven my first limo. Finally, a gypsy cab slowed down and checked me out. Dressed in a black suit, white shirt, and trenchcoat, I must have looked decent enough so soon I was on my way to Michelle's garage. When the cab driver honked his horn, a heavy metal door slowly rose, revealing three sparkling Rolls Royce Silver Spurs. There were two regular length and one double. I was anxious to get behind the wheel as I had been waiting for this moment for the past three months.

"Take whichever one you want," the dispatcher told me. "Your pick-up is at Kennedy. It's a prepaid credit-card job. The passenger will recognize the limo when you get there. You'll get instructions from the client."

The rate was $85 per hour, with a one-hour minimum, and I would get 20% of the total fare plus a 5% gratuity. I jumped in the double-length Silver Spur and started trying to figure out all the gadgets. It was an impossible task in a short time so I pulled out and headed toward Kennedy which was about twenty minutes away. From the moment I was on the road, sitting behind this luxurious piece of machinery, I knew that I was going to love this job.

The dispatcher had told me that my pick-up would be waiting at the international customs building. It was deserted outside the terminal, not a soul around. I circled around a few times, parked the limousine, and called the dispatcher who told me to look around inside the terminal. If the passenger wasn't to be found, the company still would pay me for an hour's work.

My walk around the area didn't reveal anybody who looked like they were expecting a Rolls Royce limo. Ready to head back outside, I noticed a black man sleeping in a fetal position, his body half-resting on a window ledge, head covered by the hood of his jacket. He looked like a homeless person seeking refuge from the bitter cold. But something was out of character. A very expensive-looking leather bag was lying next to him.

"Excuse me, sir. Did you order a limo?"

The man raised his head to look at me and pulled open the hood. I couldn't believe it, newly-crowned heavyweight champion Mike Tyson was staring me in the face.

"Yeah, man, I called for you. Where's the limo?" He put his hood back on and stood up. "Grab that," he said, motioning for me to pick up the Louis Vitton bag on the floor next to him.

I was very nervous because Mike Tyson was going to be my first limo passenger. I was sure I was going to fuck up and never drive a limo again in my life. Everybody knew about Tyson's incredible career during the past two years. Professional boxing is a passion where I come from, and Tyson was a fighter who grew up just down the road in the Brownsville section of Brooklyn. After last week's heavyweight championship victory over Trevor Berbick, anybody who read the paper or watched television recognized his face. But I never realized how massively built he was until I personally witnessed his bulging twenty-inch neck and tree-trunk legs.

13

Tyson told me to take him to Bentley's, a nightclub in mid-town Manhattan. He closed the glass partition separating us and talked on the phone the duration of the trip. When we arrived, Tyson jumped out and bolted into the club without a word, leaving me outside in the bitter cold for more than an hour. When he emerged, he was surrounded by a contingent of friends, everyone laughing at some joke one of them had just told.

"Yo, check out this limo," Tyson said, ushering his friends over to the curb, showing off the double-length Silver Spur. He opened the passenger door, and they all poked their heads inside ooing and aahing their approval. Then Tyson said he was tired, would hook up with them tomorrow, slid inside, and lowered the partition. "Hey, yo, drive me home now!"

"Where's home, sir?"

"Up I-95 to the Catskills. Three or four hours. When you get to Exit 78, wake me up. Then I'll tell ya' how to get to my house."

He raised the partition, and I started figuring whether I was going to be able to make it to work on time the next day. I headed for the expressway which becomes I-95 North, thinking that my Mom was right. I was going to lose my job at UPS if I did this chauffering business. There wasn't a sound from my passenger until I woke him up at Exit 78. Tyson was rested now, very polite, giving me detailed directions how to get to the town of Catskill and then to his house.

We were surrounded by nothing but woods for miles, when I made the final turn onto a narrow road which ended up at the driveway to a large white three-story colonial-style house. A fourteen-passenger, twenty-eight-foot-long grey Mercedes limousine was parked there, almost twice as long as my Rolls Royce "eight-pack." The driver was asleep behind the wheel. Mike Tyson jumped out, and I followed three steps behind him. He began banging on the driver's window. I could see the old man inside, momentarily dazed and confused. He opened the door, revealing the raspberry-colored interior. I peered back at the huge passenger compartment which had been converted into a master bedroom with a bar and television.

Tyson told his chauffeur that his co-manager, Jim Jacobs, repeatedly had attempted to reach him with no response so they had to find a limousine service in the middle of the night. The old man apologized and maintained that nobody had awakened him to tell him that his famous boss was waiting at the airport.

"Get outta' the car. Don't worry 'bout not picking me up 'cause you're fired. Give the keys to my man here."

Tyson shrugged in my direction, then headed for the house. The chauffeur followed him, apologizing and begging for his job back, but Tyson just waved him away.

"You drive for me now," Tyson said, turning to me. The old man knew by now he wasn't going to change Tyson's mind and handed me the keys to the fourteen-pack Mercedes.

I was stunned at being awarded the position of Tyson chauffeur on my first trip out as a limo driver, having only exchanged a few words with him during the past ten hours.

"Sir, I can't do that," I said without thinking. "I have

a regular job at UPS. In fact," I continued, pointing at my watch, "I'm supposed to be there in three hours. This is the first limo job I ever had."

Tyson snatched the keys back from me. I asked him if he would please sign the job ticket to confirm the total time he had used the service. He scribbled his initials on it, pulled out something from his pants pocket, and returned the ticket to me. There were three hundred dollar bills rolled up inside as a tip.

"Thank you, sir " I said and, again without thinking, handed him back the cash. "I can't take this. It was an honor just driving for you."

"Okay," he said and walked away. I went back and fetched his Louis Vitton bag. After returning it to him, I jumped back in the Rolls Royce and raced down I-95 on my way back to the City, hoping to be able to report on time to UPS. I was feeling great. Everything had gone without a hitch. I hadn't gotten lost in the Catskills or wrecked the limo, and I was going to make almost $100 for driving around the newly-crowned heavyweight champion in one of the finest luxury automobiles ever made.

When I pulled into the garage at 125th Street and Riverside Drive, Ruth was there and asked me how the job had gone. When I told her that my passenger was Mike Tyson, she got very upset. Had she known it was going to be a celebrity passenger, she would have used one of her experienced drivers. Apparently, the caller who placed the credit-card order for the job was the other Tyson co-manager, Bill Cayton, whose name didn't ring a bell with the dispatcher.

Three things occurred that cold November night which landed me the job that would change my life, and Mike Tyson's, forever: Tyson's chauffeur was nowhere to be found, Michelle's dispatcher didn't know Cayton's order involved a celebrity, and I happened to be available from the stand-by list at 3:00 a.m. the previous morning.

"Don't worry, everything went fine," I told Ruth, hoping my first drive for Michelle's wasn't going to be my last. "He even offered me a job as his chauffeur."

Ruth seemed relieved, then laughed. "Don't believe it, Rudy. Celebrities say the same thing to my drivers all the time."

Life returned to normal for me after that November trip. Nobody at UPS believed I had chauffered Mike Tyson to the Catskills and, even if I had, he certainly wasn't serious when he asked me to go work for him. The Christmas-New Years season kept me busy as a part-timer for Michelle's. It had a contract with the Park Central Hotel. I didn't get any celebrities, mostly foreign business types. And the jobs usually involved taking people to restaurants, the theater, or the opera. My ten-hour job for Mike Tyson appeared to have been a once-in-a-lifetime stroke of luck.

Just like my days at the Playboy Club, I once again was getting used to surviving on very little sleep, juggling my time between my UPS and chauffeur jobs. But I was learning how to be a professional chauffeur, the courtesies, the protocol and, to a great extent, learning how to pass the hours in the limo waiting for the clients.

On the last day of December, 1986, Ruth called me. Mike Tyson had ordered one of Michelle's limos for the whole night and insisted I be his driver, even though he had that huge fourteen-pack Mercedes. In the early afternoon, I was dispatched to Manhattan's luxurious Marlborough House at East 40th Street and Second Avenue near the United Nations to pick up Tyson's older sister, Denise, and some friends. Then I was to drive them to Tyson who was at the house in the Catskills. Denise was enormous then, weighing nearly four-hundred pounds. My passengers were very nice and polite to me during that trip and apologized for the nearly dozen times they stopped to buy junk food and sodas.

In early 1990, Denise died at age twenty-six, and I attended her funeral with my boss, Mike Tyson.

When we arrived three hours later at the house where I had taken Tyson a month before, my passengers piled out, slipping and sliding on the snow which had been accumulating on the driveway. I remained in the Rolls, awaiting further instructions. By then I had learned that it was not part of my job to bother a client about what I was supposed to do next. A few minutes later, an elderly white lady with deeply sunken cheeks carefully made her way down the driveway to the Rolls.

"I am Camille," she said, handing me a cup of hot chocolate and some chocolate-chip cookies wrapped in a paper napkin. She had a foreign accent, and I assumed that she was the live-in maid.

Later I would learn that this residence, known as "The White House," was really Camille's house which she had shared for many years with life-long companion Cus D'Amato. Cus was a boxing legend, producing several champions, including Floyd Patterson and Jose Torres. Camille Ewald and Cus D'Amato brought Tyson into their home in 1979 when he was twelve-years old. When Tyson's mother, Lorna, died in 1982 from stomach cancer, he asked Camille to be his mother and she agreed. D'Amato later formally adopted Tyson, one year before the legendary trainer died.

I hadn't yet seen my client that day as he spent several hours inside visiting with his sister and the others I had picked up at his Manhattan apartment. Finally, he emerged from The White House, accompanied only by a hulking, seven-foot, three-hundred pound black man introduced to me as Caesar, his bodyguard.

19

"Hey, yo, take us back to the City."

I don't think Mike Tyson knew my name yet. He referred to me simply as "yo" that New Years, and I respectfully called him "sir" at all times as I shuttled him and his bodyguard around Manhattan. I always called him "sir" during the four years I was at his side full-time. He eventually insisted I call him "Mike," and I said "sure" but continued calling him "sir" anyway, except on rare occasions. That New Years he and Caesar stopped off briefly at several clubs, including Studio 54 and Bentley's. As usual, I stayed outside with the limousine. Finally, he told me to head over to Jersey and asked me if I knew how to get to Englewood. He said we were going to "Sugarhill," to Eddie Murphy's place. I couldn't believe it. Things were getting even better for me in my quest for excitement. Eddie Murphy was on top of the world at that time, a mega-superstar, riding the wave of several blockbuster movies.

When we arrived at the huge estate a little before midnight, there already were dozens of limos parked outside. There was no doubt that a major bash was taking place inside. Through the picture windows I could see lots of beautiful girls running around in bikinis. Tyson left Caesar outside with me. While the party went on inside, I spent my time talking to the other chauffeurs and observed the comings and goings of the celebrities, mostly black musical personalities, among whom were Al B Sure, Bobby Brown, Run-D.M.C, and Heavy D. There weren't any white guests whom we could see, but it appeared that Murphy's entire housekeeping staff was white. Tyson sent me three times to pick up friends from his old Brownsville neighborhood. So

I ended up shuttling a total of six hours between Englewood and Brooklyn that night.

I eventually dozed off when about 11 a.m. Mike Tyson tapped on the driver's window, surrounded by three very pretty young black girls.

"Yo, where's my movies?"

Tyson always took video cassettes wherever he went. I found them on the floor in the back in an expensive designer bag and handed it to him. He showed the girls the available selection, and they finally decided on one to stick in the VCR before piling into the back of the Rolls.

"Hey, yo, take me to the Catskills," he said as the glass partition went up.

I had been on the job almost twenty-four hours, and now there would be at least another six added to this job. I didn't hear anything from my passengers until we arrived at The White House which, being my third trip there, I had no problem finding on my own. I asked Mike Tyson to sign my job ticket with these extra hours so I wouldn't get in trouble for keeping the limousine out for so long. Again, he wanted to tip me, and again I refused.

"It's no problem, sir. I'll see you next time."

He looked confused. "Yo, you don't want no money, man? What's up with you?"

Tyson insisted that I take my time getting back to the City and ordered me to add several hours more on the ticket to make sure all my time would be covered. To my surprise, he reached out and gave me a hug around the neck. It was the

21

beginning of a tradition which Tyson carried on until the very end to show his appreciation when I handled a job for him respectfully and professionally.

"I'll call you when I need you."

I noticed that the fourteen-pack Mercedes limo still was parked in the driveway in the exact same spot it had been that first night back in November.

Almost three months went by without Mike Tyson requesting me as his driver. At the White House on New Year's Day, he had said he would call when he needed me. I figured he must have come into the City dozens of times during that period. I remembered what Ruth had told me after my first Tyson job, that celebrities are always making promises they never intend to keep. Both my jobs were slowing down after the holiday season. I got a few calls from Michelle's for airport runs. And there had been one communication from my famous passenger. The dispatcher called one day and said that Tyson had requested I pick up a white male named Jay Bright and take him around Manhattan for some sightseeing and shopping. Jay had been one of the troubled "foster" kids, like Tyson, whom Cus and Camille cared for at The White House.

On March 7, 1987, Mike Tyson beat "Bonecrusher" Smith at the Las Vegas Hilton, adding the WBA heavyweight title to his WBC title. A few weeks after that I received a message at UPS to call Michelle's. At that time I was working the 6 a.m. to 3 p.m. shift, mostly sorting packages.

"Mike Tyson called and wants you to pick up one of the Rolls and go to Atlantic City." I could tell by her tone that she was upset with this job order.

"Is there a problem?"

"The problem is, we've got a system here. A seniority system. I've got drivers sitting around doing nothing with a lot more experience than you, especially for top clients. And you've got another full-time job anyway."

"If you've got a problem, discuss it with Mike Tyson."

Ruth didn't respond for a few moments. Then she said that there was a clean Rolls Royce ready for me and hung up.

By 4:00 p.m. I was heading down the Jersey Turnpike with the Atlantic City address where Mike Tyson was staying. I let the doorman at the Ocean Club know who I was, and he assured me he would let Mr. Tyson know right away that I had arrived. Two hours later Mike Tyson descended from the penthouse and gave me that same hug around the neck. Then we headed out for some shopping, accompanied by an entourage of Tyson's friends visiting from his old neighborhood. He seemed very relaxed and happy that afternoon.

I had to call UPS and request time off because that one afternoon turned into three full days. When I called Michelle's to let them know how long the job was going to take, Ruth got on the line. Again she sounded upset. She had a rule that drivers had to check in every hour, and I hadn't been in touch for half a day. And then she became very agitated, accusing me of "negotiating" the extended job directly with Mike Tyson when that business decision wasn't mine to be made. She started rambling about splitting up twenty-four hours of work among three drivers. Ruth wasn't making any sense, and I couldn't understand why she was complaining. The prestigious client was happy with me, and this job meant non-stop income for her company for the several days it lasted. I wasn't about to burden Mike Tyson with Ruth's rules and hangups. I said I had to get going and hung up.

At the end of the third day, Tyson asked me to run one of his visiting friends back to Brooklyn and turn in the limo. He gave me the customary hug, told me to add six hours as a tip, signed the ticket, and said he'd call when he got back to the City. Because I figured I couldn't count on Ruth to give me anymore jobs, especially for Mike Tyson, I had left my beeper number with him in Atlantic City. One afternoon in May I got a call on the job around 2:00 p.m. I called the number on the pager. It was Mike Tyson calling from the White House in Catskill.

"Yo, I want a limo up at my house by 8:00 p.m."

I got on the phone to Ruth right away to book a Rolls Royce for Mike Tyson. She wanted to know why a client was dealing directly with me. It was clear she was putting an end to this procedure. She was tired of his requesting one particular driver because that's not the way things worked around there.

I gave her the number to The White House. "You call him if you've got a problem with me taking the job," I said, and hung up.

She told me that's exactly what she was going to do.

An hour later, Al Salvy, the hub manager, came to see me. We weren't on very good terms by that time. I had received several promotions and now was in charge of PD1, supervising all deliveries into Brooklyn. Rivalries and dislike among the various ethnic groups, blacks, Puerto Ricans, anglos, orientals, was a way of life in the City, and UPS was no different. But I did everything I could to turn our cultural mix into a team. I tried to be fair and flexible and covered for the guys

25

I supervised when they had emergencies or family problems. Everybody worked their asses off. We had zero "service failures" for three consecutive months, meaning no packages got lost or delivered late during that period. Salvy didn't like the way I got along with everybody because that wasn't normal. He was convinced that I wanted his job.

"Gonzalez, I'm sick and tired of people calling you up," Salvy barked at me. "You waste a lot of company time with that chauffeur bullshit. Now there's somebody on the line impersonating Mike Tyson."

"It *is* Mike Tyson."

"Yeah, right," he said, giving me the finger as he turned and walked away.

I went to Salvy's office and pressed the button of the flashing line.

"Yo, what's up with that bitch at the limo office?"

"Sir, I don't have any control over the company rules."

"I'm tired of this bullshit," Tyson said. "What are you doin'?"

"Sir, I don't get off for another hour. What do you want me to do?"

There was a short pause. Then Tyson said: "I'll work out something else for right now. You quit your job and come work for me. Go down later to the heliport at 34th and East River Drive. They got a chopper waitin' for ya'."

Then there was a click as Mike Tyson hung up. I looked around Al Salvy's office. There was a certificate on the wall showing appreciation for twenty-five years of faithfull service. I saw myself going nowhere. Maybe if I were lucky I would be standing in my boss' shoes twenty-five years down the road, tired and bitter. A helicopter was waiting for me. I asked myself what was I waiting for. I picked up the phone, called my Mom, and told her Mike Tyson had offered me a job. She wasn't happy with the prospect, my giving up a good job for something that didn't have a future. She had watched my paychecks from work increase steadily. My Dad was still doing time in Sing Sing, and she wanted me to have a safe and stable life.

I strolled around the UPS building for a few minutes, realizing I wasn't ever going to be head of a big company like United Parcel Service. Ruth had burned my bridge to Mike Tyson. She wasn't giving me any other work either. I was at the dead end of my exciting part-time career.

I found my boss sitting in the cafeteria taking his afternoon break and announced that I was quitting.

"What's your fucking problem now, Gonzalez?"

"Mike Tyson offered me a job."

He shook his head and raised his eyes to the ceiling. "Would you please stop the fucking bullshit."

"I'm outta' here," I said and walked away.

Salvy was both shocked and mad. There wasn't anybody to replace me right away. I went to say goodbye to the employees who were loading and sorting packages for me. When they heard the news, they cheered and slapped me on the back. I hurried back to the apartment in Spanish Harlem and packed a small bag. In the taxi on the way to the heliport, I began feeling regret and insecurity. What the fuck was I doing? I had quit a good-paying supervisor's job in a big company. I had no idea how much I was going to earn working for Mike Tyson, or for how long this job was supposed to last. It also dawned on me that I was going to work for somebody who didn't even know my name, still calling me "yo" six months after I first met him early that cold November morning.

"The Jacket"

Donald Trump recently had acquired Pan Am's helicopter service, adding it to his collection of real-estate and hotel properties. The business operated from a heliport at 34th Street and East River Drive. The taxi pulled up to a construction trailer which served as Trump Air's mini-terminal. Several helicopters were parked nearby, bearing the logos of local tv stations. I entered the trailer and told the lady behind the counter that I was going to Atlantic City, that Mike Tyson was supposed to have made advance arrangements for me.

"Oh, yes, you must be Mr. Gonzalez," she said with a big smile. "Your helicopter is en route. And," she added, reaching underneath the counter and producing a big white box. "Mr. Tyson left something for you."

A moment later there was a tremendous roar which violently shook the trailer.

"Mr. Gonzalez, there you go," the woman shouted over the noise, pointing toward the door.

Setting down delicately was an enormous black Huey helicopter marked "TRUMP." A hostess saw me and beckoned me in. When the doors closed, the deafening roar suddenly was replaced by total silence.

"Please fasten your seatbelt, Mr. Gonzalez."

A moment later we lifted off, swinging out at a 45-degree angle and heading west over Manhattan toward the Hudson River. I was the only passenger. The chopper's interior was filled with elegant wrap-around couches, and huge gold "T's" were displayed throughout. I realized then that this had to be Donald Trump's private helicopter.

The hostess asked me if I would like something to eat and drink so I ordered a Coke and a bag of peanuts. Again I asked myself, "what the fuck am I doing here?" But for the moment there wasn't much I could do at 8,000 feet, the enormous power of the Huey hurtling us toward Atlantic City. I sat back and sunk into the plush dark-chocolate leather. The hostess got on a phone to Atlantic City and began making arrangements. I decided to open the large white box Tyson had left for me at the Trump Air counter. Inside there was a red-white-and-blue leather Tyson fight jacket. On the back it read "World-Heavyweight Champion" and had Tyson's face hand-stitched in shades of leather to create a detailed image. Later I would learn that the jacket was crafted by leather-apparel-maker-to-the-stars, Jeff Hamilton and was valued at over $5,000. I kept staring at the jacket's incredible beauty. Then I turned it over. I now realized that Mike Tyson really did know my name. On the front, embroidered in big letters was "RUDY."

Before we landed in Atlantic City, the hostess told me I was getting a quick sightseeing tour of the area. She showed me some of the hotels, including those where Tyson had crushed four of twenty-eight opponents during his undefeated meteroic rise to heavyweight champion in less than two years. Resorts International where he knocked out Donnie Long in the first round, the Atlantis where he disposed of Robert Colay also in the first, and the Trump Plaza where he polished off Mike Jameson in the fifth and Jose Ribalta in the tenth. Then she pointed out a thirty-story pyramid-shaped luxury condominium building. It was the Ocean Club where Mike Tyson resided in the penthouse.

As the Huey touched down near the Trump Regent, in the distance I could see a huge hole where construction on the next Trump hotel, The Taj Mahal, was underway. When the chopper's doors dropped down, I was greeted by four big black guys, including Tyson's bodyguard, Caesar. I noticed a small crowd waiting nearby, expecting to catch a glimpse of "The Donald." Instead they got the Puerto Rican kid from UPS. Caesar grabbed my hand, shook it warmly, and introduced the others, Jaymore, Ouie, and Bill.

As we made our way toward his car, Caesar tapped me on the shoulder. "You're part of the team now."

Caesar introduced me to the doorman and some of the other personnel at the Ocean Club, informing them that I now was part of the official Tyson crew. Things were moving too fast for me. I was curious why Mike Tyson suddenly had placed such great confidence in me, making me part of his official "team."

31

Later I would learn that Mike Tyson had sensed in me something unusual. I always had been very respectful and business-like, keeping my distance, even though I had gotten to know him better after so many hours chauffeuring him around. On that first trip in November 1986, when I picked Tyson up at Kennedy Airport and took him to Bentley's night-club in Manhattan, ending up ten hours later at The White House in Catskill, New York, I had refused a $300 tip. I had told him that it was an honor just driving him around. Again I refused a big tip the next time I served as his chauffeur that New Year's Eve. And Mike Tyson came to understand that I wasn't interested in his money. After he became wealthy and famous, there had been very few people like me in Tyson's life.

"Let's go up," Caesar said after taking me around. "MT's waiting to see you."

We got into a private key-access-only express elevator that whisked us to the penthouse floor. The living room had a glass ceiling which gave it the effect of a crystal palace. Everything was done in white, rugs, furniture, huge marble sculptures, and there were pillows stitched in gold. Portraits of the fighter hung on the walls. It was very quiet inside, servants coming and going without making a sound.

In the middle of the living room, Mike Tyson sat back on a beautiful white leather sofa, dressed only in lycra athletic shorts, a diamond Rolex dangling from his wrist, his ruby-and-diamond clustered WBC Championship ring reflecting sunlight which poured through the glass roof. Tyson was speaking on a portable phone in a low voice. He

32

saw me and waved me in, indicating I should grab a seat.

Before that day, I had no idea what it was like to smell and taste such enormous wealth and power. Sure, I had met people with money while driving for Ruth's limo service. I had seen the inside of a number of fine hotels, apartment buildings, and restaurants. But that day, after my ride in Donald Trump's personal helicopter embellished with gold "T"s, and now sitting in this palace penthouse, I realized a few lucky people enjoyed a level of wealth and power far beyond my imagination.

Tyson looked over at me, put his hand over the receiver, and reached out to shake my hand. "You did it, right?"

I nodded sheepishly, and he grinned widely in response. He ended his phone conversation and snapped his fingers. A tall black man, the butler, appeared from nowhere.

"Rudy's gonna' drive my shit. Make sure you take care of him."

I got up, expecting to follow the butler, but my new boss motioned for me to remain seated.

"Relax, enjoy yourself. It's going to be fun for you. We need a limo. We've gotta' buy some limos. I fired all my drivers. I had them all over the place. They're all fired. You're my driver now. You're gonna' be in full control and in charge of all my cars. You're gonna' travel with me wherever I go."

He told Caesar that Ouie had to move out and go to a hotel. Instead, I would take over his bedroom. He also instructed Caesar to take me downstairs, show me around town, and buy me all the clothes I needed for the next two weeks.

"No need for you to go back to the City now."

Ouie, one of Tyson's closest childhood friends from Brownsville, later told me that I must be pretty important to get him kicked out of that bedroom.

Before Caesar and I made it to the door, Tyson called out. "And Caesar, take Rudy down to the garage later. I don't even know what I got. Everybody's been playing around with my shit. Go downstairs and straighten my shit out. Make it pretty."

In the elevator descending to the lobby, Caesar said: "Listen, Rudy, everything is a mess. But don't worry about it right now. Let's get you some clothes first."

We went to the garage to get Caeser's jeep, and I asked him which of the array of luxury cars belonged to my new boss.

Caesar chuckled. "They *all* belong to MT."

I couldn't believe it, expecting that Tyson owned maybe two or three cars besides the grey fourteen-pack Mercedes. Instead, Caesar pointed out twenty expensive vehicles, all dirty, some with flats, others with body damage. I told Caesar that I wanted to go right away to an auto supply store and buy shampoo, wax, and detailing items. He reminded me that first Tyson wanted me to get some clothes and become familiar with Atlantic City. But I protested loudly, and Caesar finally gave in.

When we returned thirty minutes later, I took off my shirt and got to work washing, waxing, and cleaning Tyson's automobile collection and also organizing everything I found inside, including dozens of audio and video cassettes. Six hours later, Mike Tyson came looking for me, dressed in his favorite white sweat shorts. I heard him yelling my name as he entered the garage with Caesar.

"Rudy, what are you doin'?"

"I'm getting it all together, sir."

"Forget it. Don't do that shit all at once. Come on and hang out with us."

"No, I want to finish the job."

Tyson turned to Caesar. "You see, first day on job, and he's taking care of everything."

I worked until about 2 a.m. that morning. I didn't want to stop until the job was done. I wanted my new boss to see everything clean and sparkling by morning. Finally, I made it to the bedroom and was ready to conk out. Within the past twelve hours, I had quit my supervisor's job at UPS, flown in Donald Trump's private chopper to Atlantic City, been hired formally by Mike Tyson to be his driver wherever he went, and cleaned and waxed his entire inventory of luxury automobiles. Caesar heard me next door and came in.

"You better get some rest, Rudy," he said. "MT gets up at five to go running. You've gotta' follow us in case we need the car."

At 5 a.m. sharp Caesar shook me and told me to hurry up. Tyson was already in his sweats anxious to hit the street. Caesar told me to grab the keys to one of the cars in the garage and meet them in front of the building. I threw on some clothes and jumped in the express elevator. The black Jaguar looked pretty inviting so I fired it up and sped up the ramp to street level. Tyson already was half-way down the street with Caesar not far behind.

The sun hadn't yet risen before Tyson finished five miles at a brisk pace. When we returned to the penthouse, Chef Early was cooking away in the kitchen. He was a tall, white-haired, very distinguished black man in his sixties whose specialty was soul food. Chef Early had cooked for many celebrities, including Michael Jackson and Whitney Houston. For breakfast, he typically served up a variety of eggs along with low-fat turkey sausages and assorted fruits and juices. Tyson would have a big breakfast, including without fail a bowl of his favorite cereal, Captain Crunch, and then go back to sleep until 11 a.m. In the late afternoon he would hit the gym and do his boxing workout. And in the evening he would spend some time on the treadmill, stair-master, gravitron, or stationary bike. I soon learned that this was the regimen that Mike Tyson followed and enjoyed and which, by the time I started working for him, had made him the heavyweight champion of the world.

Caesar told me I was dismissed until MT woke up at 11 a.m. so I headed down to the garage, applied Armorall to the vinyl and leather surfaces of all the cars, and made a list of broken items I had discovered the night before.

Tyson was standing behind me in shorts and sneakers, shaking his head in disbelief because his collection was clean, shiny, and organized for the first time since he could remember. I showed him that all his compact discs, audio and video cassettes, and even packs of chewing gum, had been organized and placed in one bag so that he could take everything with him in any of the cars at anytime.

"I can't believe this." He slapped me on the back so hard he almost knocked me down. "You know how to drive a stick?"

He told me to pull out the red Lamborghini Countach. When I started it up, it sounded like a small jet.

"We're goin' to the City, baby, for the afternoon."

I tried to let the clutch out slowly, but I had no idea of the massive power of the Countach's twelve cylinders and five-hundred horses. It sprang forward uncontrollably, and when I slammed on the brakes it died. I apologized to my boss, but Tyson just laughed, assuring me I'd get the hang of it. As we surfaced from the garage, several people saw us and shouted "Mike, Mike!" I grabbed the Jersey Turnpike and headed for New York. At Tyson's insistence we drove 90 miles per hour all the way and never got stopped. Mike Tyson loved travelling on the road at high speeds. We were in mid-town Manhattan in little over an hour.

On Madison Avenue, Tyson visited several stores while I remained with the Countach. We then headed for his old neighborhood. As we cruised slowly through the streets of the Brownsville section of Brooklyn, people screamed out his name. He told me to stop from time to time so he could get out and visit with old friends on the stoops of housing projects. We also made a stop at Brownsville Park where he ran into childhood acquaintances. I noticed many times he handed out cash. After about five hours in the City, Tyson told me he was tired. He was in training for the Pinklon Thomas fight to be held at the Las Vegas Hilton. Soon we were roaring down the Jersey Turnpike back to Atlantic City and the penthouse at the Ocean Club.

Mike Tyson's life was healthy and organized during those first few months I was with him in Atlantic City. Kevin Rooney, his main trainer already for a number of years, was a strict disciplinarian who made sure his fighter was in bed by a certain hour and followed a carefully-planned diet. When Tyson had an 11 p.m. curfew, Rooney would be at our door at 11:15 p.m. to check for compliance. If I didn't get my boss in on time, I would get yelled at. Once, when Rooney suspected that Tyson was sneaking snacks at night, we came home one evening to find a chain and lock around the refrigerator and a note taped to it: "Sorry, Mike, not until 8 a.m." Sometimes Rooney would leave his fighter a pitcher of ice water and an apple or pear with a note: "Love, Kevin."

Even though his role was full-time "enforcer," it was clear that Rooney genuinely cared about Mike Tyson. After training sessions, Rooney went beyond the call of duty, swinging by for long talks with his charge. Often he would bring movies from the local video store, with unbuttered and unsalted popcorn, if he detected that his young fighter was down or bored. He tried to be like a brother to his fighter. If we let Rooney down, we felt bad because he was such a kind and good man. He instilled a sense of "team playing" for all who worked with him. And the team was playing for the single goal of making Michael Gerard Tyson undisputed heavyweight champion of the world.

As time passed, I learned that there was a very real tradition behind the Tyson fight jacket left for me at Trump Air the day I quit my job at UPS. Kevin Rooney represented that tradition, started by Cus D'Amato in 1979. That was the year D'Amato rescued twelve-year-old Tyson from the Tryon School, part of the New York State Corrections Department, and took him into his home with Camille Ewald in Catskill, New York. Kevin Rooney was to be one of the last of those who carried on the tradition before things started going bad for Mike Tyson.

I never had the opportunity to meet Cus D'Amato because he died from pneumonia on November 4, 1985, almost exactly one year before I met Mike Tyson. But being with Tyson and his team every day, it wasn't long before I felt like I personally had known this man. In the gym, Rooney and the other two trainers, Matt Baransky and Steve Lott, would recall what D'Amato would have said about whatever issue of training or technique was troubling them. And outside the gym, when Rooney, and others who had known Cus, would be sitting around talking about things in general, their conversation frequently would be interwoven with his wisdoms.

I don't know whether the character "Mickey" in Stallone's *Rocky* movie was based in part on D'Amato's life, but there were a lot of similarities. D'Amato fell in love with boxing as a child and made it his life-long career. In the thirties, he was a boxing coach in the army. He lived for more than three decades at the Gramercy Gym, located on Fourteenth Street near Manhattan's Union Square, while Ukranian- born Camille Ewald, his companion for almost a half-century, maintained a separate home in upstate New York. The

Gramercy Gym produced champions Rocky Graziano, Floyd Patterson, and Jose Torres, the last two trained by Cus D'Amato.

D'Amato suffered from a number of physical ailments during most of his life. At the age of twelve-years, the same age he informally adopted Mike Tyson, D'Amato got into a street fight and injured his right eye from which he never would see clearly again. By early middle-age, he practically had lost the ability to smell and taste. D'Amato also was color-blind. But he had a strong will and was a workaholic, an unrelenting drill seargent dedicated to pushing his boxing students to perfection. It was from D'Amato that Tyson got into the habit of a 5 a.m. five-mile jog, an afternoon training session, and an evening workout on the machines. He also was fearless, standing up at great personal risk to mobsters Frankie Carbo and Blinky Palermo who had attempted to wedge themselves into the world of professional boxing. That was why he had developed the irritating habit of constantly looking over his shoulder in restaurants and other public places.

After years at the Gramercy Gym, D'Amato finally moved to the Catskills to live full-time with Camille. They had decided to purchase an old house next to the Hudson River in the sleepy town of Catskill. The residence had three-stories and seven bedrooms, and it wasn't long before they began taking in troubled kids to fill the house, especially those in whom D'Amato saw a potential professional fighter. Two miles away, above the police station on Main Street, D'Amato had set up the only gym in the area to teach kids the sport of boxing.

Fate would have it that in 1978 the State of New York decided to transfer unrepentant, multiple-offender Michael Gerard Tyson out of the City's Spofford detention center to the Tryon School, a much-harsher reformatory in Johnstown. Despite the severe discipline imposed on the young inmates, Tyson continued out of control until one day he noticed a poster of a boxer on the wall of the school's gym. He realized that the school's athletic coach, Bobby Stewart, was that man. After promising, and then proving, to Stewart that he would change his ways, the former professional welterweight agreed to give Tyson some lessons.

It didn't take long for Stewart to conclude that his young student was somebody with extraordinary raw talent and physical ability. He took Tyson on to visit Cus D'Amato in nearby Catskill. A short time later, D'Amato was negotiating with the New York State Corrections Department to get the boy released to his custody. In 1979, the youngster went to live at The White House along with other troubled youths taken in by Cus and Camille. From that point on, D'Amato shaped Tyson into the winner of the 1984 National Golden Gloves competition and, later, a professional heavyweight champion who by the time I met him was unbeaten in twenty-eight bouts, twenty-six of which were by knockouts.

Mike Tyson didn't have a relationship with Jimmy Kirkpatrick, his natural father who never lived with him. Cus D'Amato filled that role by bringing Tyson into his home to live with him, Camille Ewald, and the other "sons." One year before his death, D'Amato became his legal guardian. After Tyson's mother, Lorna, died of cancer in 1982, Tyson asked Camille to become his mother. She tells the story that one afternoon her "son" brought home a friend and introduced her as his mother. The kid looked at Tyson, then at her, then back at Tyson, shaking his head and walking away confused. Tyson also had a number of "brothers" during those years at The White House, Jay Bright, Tom Patti, and others to whom Cus and Camille had opened their doors. There is a home video of them sitting around the dining table, and you can see in Mike Tyson's expression how happy he was to be a part of this multi-racial family.

D'Amato believed that the real power of the fighter was in the mind more than the fists. That's why he spent so much time speaking with the youngster who came to live with him in 1979. He needed to find out what was going on inside that very disturbed head, praying that he could redirect all the negative energy to the sport of boxing, and in the process to save the kid from a life of crime and premature death. His talks with Tyson, as well as with others whom he guided over the years, included his admonition that too much money and woman-chasing were evils which destroyed the strength and purity of the professional athlete.

Cus D'Amato was convinced from the first day that Bobby Stewart brought young Mike Tyson to him that he had a future heavyweight champion on his hands. And so from the very beginning, Cus carefully surrounded Tyson with those who shared D'Amato's values and beliefs, and who had

Tyson's welfare, both personal and professional, as their number one concern. This was the tradition started by Cus D'Amato in 1979, a tradition embodied in my Tyson fight jacket given to me in 1987. It wasn't about money. We were a family. The first year I served Mike Tyson, very few conversations in his life revolved around money. Sadly, this tradition was to come to a close within a couple of years. During my first year of service, Tyson seemed to take his fabulous earnings in stride. He would enjoy travelling back often to his old Brownsville neighborhood, sitting on tenement stoops or in the park, joking with old friends.

"Treat people right," he told me. "Don't let this shit get to you." He was referring to his money, luxury cars, and other possessions.

Mike Tyson was very concerned about the living conditions of black people in this country, especially the children, and wanted to do something about it.

"What is important is caring about people. Even if I got a billion dollars, I'm still gonna' be known as little Ike." It was his way of saying that he would never grow larger than life.

If MT saw people on the street who looked desperate, he would tell me to stop, bolt out of the limo, and hand them some cash. He never carried anything less than $100 bills. I observed him hand out $100 bills to hundreds of kids. We would get the cash at Bill Cayton's office on 40th Street after signing receipts to keep track of the outflow. I would sit in MT's apartment and use paperclips to divide the bills into $1,000 packs so he would know how much dough he had with him.

44

On the average, Mike Tyson would carry around $25,000 in cash in case he wanted to stop and buy something. He was an impulse buyer. One summer day in 1987, we were on Atlantic Avenue in Brooklyn, and we passed by A.J. Lester's sporting goods store. He told me to stop the limo, and he went inside and bought ten dozen pair of sneakers of all sizes. We loaded up the limo and drove around the Brownsville section of Brooklyn, handing them out to the kids on the street. Tyson also liked to park the limo and play with the kids. During that first summer I remember we had a lot of spontaneous touch football games.

This is when Tyson seemed happiest during the years I worked for him. He wanted to make people feel he was just a normal guy from the neighborhood who had never forgotten his people. It didn't bother Tyson back then that the media might not appreciate the fact he wasn't doing a whole lot of glamorous things.

One day approximately eight months after I started working full-time for MT, he turned to me.

"Hey, man, have I ever paid you?"

Although all of my basic needs, food, clothing, shelter, transportation, had been taken care of, I never had received a paycheck during that time.

"No, sir, we never discussed this. I don't know if I'm getting paid by you."

He looked over at me in amazement. This was further proof to him that I wasn't after his money. After that day, I was placed on the payroll at $300 a week. My first check included all the time since I had come aboard full-time in May of 1987.

Some of the team fashioned by D'Amato still was with Tyson when I started in May of 1987. There were trainers Kevin Rooney, Matt Baransky, and Steve Lott. There were Jim Jacobs and Bill Cayton who had co-managed Tyson and developed a game plan which propelled him from amateur to world champion in less than two years and made him a very rich man by age twenty. Jacobs was a former champion handball player and long-time D'Amato friend who was a collector, first of comic books, then of fight films, owning the world's largest collection. Over the years, Mike Tyson spent hundreds of hours in his attic room at The White House studying these films. When Cus died at the end of 1985, Jacobs became the man in whom Mike Tyson placed his greatest trust until Jacobs himself died in the spring of 1988.

As his health rapidly deteriorated in the mid-eighties, Cus D'Amato used to say that the only reason he had to keep on living was to see the day when Mike Tyson would become heavyweight champion of the world. He passed away before that day came, but he was able to witness his "son" win eleven professional fights, all by knockouts. But the aging trainer, who had made Tyson the unbeatable heavyweight machine he was, never took credit for his success.

"I just discover and uncover," D'Amato used to say about his fighters. "They do all the rest."

On May 30, 1987, Mike Tyson was set to fight Pinklon Thomas at the Las Vegas Hilton. The match was to be Tyson's defense of both the WBC and WBA heavyweight titles. Because there was still a lot to do to put the inventory of cars back in mint condition, MT decided to leave me in Atlantic City. In the sixth round, Tyson ko'd the challenger and was back at the Ocean Club the following day.

Things were quiet for the next two months because another fight at the Hilton was scheduled less than two months away, against the IBF heavyweight champion, Tony Tucker. So Kevin Rooney had MT back on a tight leash, calling revelie each day at 5 a.m. to suit up for the morning run. In the afternoons, Rooney and the other trainers would get Tyson on the light and heavy bags and then watch him spar with partners, James Broad, Mike Williams, Oscar Holman, Walter Santemore, Mike Jameson, and Licous Kirkley.

Part of the training session included specialized techniques created by Cus D'Amato. One of the techniques was to develop Tyson's trademark rapidfire bobbing and weaving. Because Tyson was shorter than many heavyweights, Cus knew he would have to be able to "hide out" for a time, bobbing and weaving from side to side, until he could get in close enough to employ uppercut or roundhouse punches with devastating effect. Rooney would tie a golf ball to a long string, then suspend it from the ceiling. Setting it in motion like a pendulum, MT would have to quickly move from side to side and up and down to avoid getting bopped on the head. Rooney would pick up the speed and send it in different directions, and Tyson would dip, bob, and weave faster and faster. It drove me crazy watching that ball for hours swinging all over the place. Training methods, such as this one, seemed to give Tyson an edge over his opponents.

The Ocean Club had an exercise room with treadmills, stationary bikes, stairmasters, and a gravitron machine. Rooney would swing by at night and make sure Tyson faithfully was performing his evening workout. Obesity ran in Tyson's family which caused everybody to be concerned, including my boss, about unchecked weight gain. Tyson's older brother, Rodney, weighed 280 pounds by age eleven, and his sister, Denise, died from an obesity-related heart attack in her mid-twenties. Rooney and the other trainers meticulously calculated the proper daily caloric intake for their charge and worked closely with the cook to develop low-fat meals. Chef Early whipped up a lot of inventive turkey dishes. I could see the pained expression on MT's face whenever he saw tv commercials showing barbecued ribs, cheeseburgers, or fried chicken. But as long as he had his "CK," Captain Crunch, cereal every morning, life was bearable. He ate it dry, and it made his stomach feel very full.

Rooney soon began to realize that, as his chauffeur, I was going everywhere with Tyson. He pulled me aside one day, instructing me to report to him if MT wanted to do something that would violate the strict training program. But at that time Tyson usually was happy just relaxing after each of his three workouts, listening to music or watching videos. He had all of Billie Holiday's recordings and also an extensive rap music collection. Most of his videos were martial arts movies and cartoons. His favorite movies were *Fists of Fury* and *The Flying Ninjas,* and his favorite cartoons were "Tom and Jerry" and "The Roadrunner."

Co-managers, Bill Cayton and Jim Jacobs, would meet with Tyson from time to time, explaining his financial situation and the steps they had taken to protect his wealth and well-being. If they needed him to pay certain bills, they would sit with him and explain in detail the reason for the expenditure. They also made me aware that no craziness was allowed in the Tyson camp, and that all members of the team were working toward the same goal, to ensure that Mike Tyson's career kept moving ahead on a safe and profitable course.

When I wasn't chauffering him around, I spent a lot of time taking care of his cars, making sure his shit was in order. Tyson seemed pleased with what was happening with his car collection. Before I joined the team, he had trouble saying no. With me now in charge of all of MT's cars, he told everybody they had to check with me first. I would tell whomever wanted to use one of the cars that there was something wrong with it. This way very few cars ever left the garage unless driven by me or Mike. This system seemed to give great relief to Tyson who hated saying "no" to friends and family. It was easy for me.

Two months later, Tyson returned to Vegas where he won a decision against Tony Tucker whose goal was just to survive twelve rounds in the ring with "Iron Mike." This added the IBF heavyweight title to the other two titles, the WBC and WBA. He now was the proud owner of the belts from all three recognized boxing associations.

Although he seemed to appreciate my hard work, professionalism, and courtesy, there were times that Mike Tyson yelled at me during our stay in Atlantic City. For one thing, he didn't like repeating directions or instructions. But by then I had met enough rich people to realize that in general they don't have much patience for anything. I also knew that most rich people yell at their help from time to time because it is part of a power display they feel necessary to prevent people from taking advantage of them or sometimes to impress others.

I didn't let it get to me. Mike Tyson had treated me kindly on a daily basis long enough for me to know that I was appreciated. Once in awhile, when things really got to him, I would see him down in the garage inspecting the cars, looking for dirt or other problems with his "fleet." He never found what he was looking for. Sometimes he would storm away, mumbling, "Man, I can't ever get anything on you."

Kevin Rooney always reminded me of one of Cus D'Amato's sayings. "Don't do what the champion wants you to do, just do what's right for the champion."

During the more than six years I worked for him, Mike Tyson fired me twice for refusing to obey instructions. I had refused because what he asked me to do was against his best interests. Each time MT hired me back right away. By putting his welfare above all else, he realized I had become

50

a true member of the tradition started by Cus D'Amato in 1979 when he took into his home a black kid from Brownsville with no future to make him a champion of the world. That tradition was carried on by those whom Cus assembled to carry the dream forward even after he was gone. And that was the tradition represented by The Jacket bearing my name.

"Gotta Have It" Given$

As Mike Tyson continued to earn increasingly fabulous sums of money, the anxiety level of his co-managers, Jim Jacobs and Bill Cayton, went up accordingly. While the fighter was in training, the strict D'Amato-Rooney regimen kept him in check. Between March 6 and December 27, 1985, Tyson had fifteen heavyweight matches, an average of 1.5 fights per month. Between January 11 and November 22, 1986, he fought thirteen times, an average of more than one each month. The result was that in less than two years, Mike Tyson had severely depleted the stable of heavyweight boxers. There weren't many kids left on the block. Consequently, in 1987 he only had four fights, during which he picked up the WBA and IBF titles.

To his co-managers, the more free time the champion had on his hands, the more likely he was to get into trouble. Now that Tyson was rich and famous, his face now recognized everywhere in every corner of the world, Jacobs and Cayton were very concerned about the "groupie syndrome." They were afraid that Tyson wouldn't be able to handle all of the new-found attention and affection. They made it clear to me and Caesar that part of our jobs was to protect Tyson from the multitudes of crazy women and gold diggers who, by being able to get close enough to the champ, would find ways to derail his career.

We were supposed to be close by at all times, even while he was having sex. I wasn't into voyeurism, but Jacobs and Cayton explained that unfortunately the truth was whatever a judge or jury *believed*, not necessarily what really *happened.*

So to help protect Tyson from false accusations and frivolous lawsuits, he always needed somebody to be with him, to observe what really was going on. The presence of another person also sent a message to Tysons' companions. Don't try to invent stories because we're here too, just outside the door, even looking in on you from time to time. I must have been in depositions half a dozen times to testify about what I witnessed between MT and groupie sex. After I testified, these cases never were pursued. Mike Tyson didn't need a chauffeur or bodyguard as much as he needed a witness.

Tyson had mentioned to us that when he was a youngster, girls used to be scared of him and run away. He never had a girlfriend while growing up in Brownsville and "never got any pussy." Now that he had money, it wasn't just his co-managers who believed women were trying to take advantage of him. He told me that "all women were alike," after his money instead of him. He wanted a relationship in which a girl wanted him instead of his money.

When I came on board in May of 1987, he was mainly seeing three black women, Naomi Campbell, Suzette Charles, and Robin Givens. Campbell was one of the world's top models who lived in a luxurious Manhattan penthouse. Charles was a former Miss America who lived in Cherry Hill, New Jersey. She was born of a mixed marriage, her father was a white, Atlantic City political figure. Robin Givens was a television actress starring in the sitcom *Head of the Class.*

"Don't let the girls cross paths," Bill Cayton warned me. Cayton believed that a tug-of-war was underway among these three ladies for the prize of Mike Tyson as their exclusive possession. Like Jacobs, Cayton was afraid a cat fight might break out if these three women got too close to each other at one of the matches. So one of my jobs was to make sure seating for each was sufficiently distant from the others.

I chauffeured Mike Tyson and Naomi Campbell around dozens of times during 1987. They were a strange mix. She was very polished, having been raised and educated in London. In her crisp British accent, she talked down to Tyson all the time, trying to "educate" him, correcting his grammar and teaching him manners. She also got him into a designer-clothes mentality by taking him on expensive shopping trips in mid-town Manhattan, to expensive boutiques on Madison and Fifth Avenues. Until then, he had been wearing clothes mostly bought at A.J. Lester's, a sporting-goods store in Brooklyn. Naomi Campbell got him into Gianni Versace, the designer for whom she did most of her modeling work. Later, his wardrobe was almost exclusively made by Versace, including $2,500 sports shirts and $5,000 leather pants. Tyson would shower her with very expensive gold and diamond jewelry.

There were a number of times I picked up Naomi Campbell from Philadelphia International, the closest major airport to Atlantic City. She was on a tight schedule so, instead of having time for a real date, many times I would just chauffeur them to Manhattan. This gave them several hours to have sex in the back of the limousine. The movement they generated in the back of the limousine was incredible.

Sometimes I thought the car, rocking and rolling, might tip over. Once we arrived at her apartment building, they would say their goodbyes.

"You know, Mike, if it wasn't for the sex, I wouldn't even talk to you," she seemed to enjoy telling him. "You don't offer me anything else."

And Tyson would just laugh. Exhausted from the non-stop sex, MT would sleep all the way back to the Ocean Club.

Campbell thoroughly enjoyed Tyson's aggressiveness those times in the back of the limousine. I had heard enough hours of her screams and shrieks of ecstasy to be certain of that. As I drove them from Atlantic City to Manhattan, MT transported her to a different planet, a world far away from that which she was accustomed to in her profession, a lot of polite, refined people, not known for their sexual prowess. Eventually Naomi Campbell got bored, and Tyson began focusing more of his attention on the two remaining significant others in his life at that point in time.

Suzette Charles was a stark contrast to the tall, black supermodel from England. Suzette was more caring and understanding when she was with Tyson. Although a very nice apple-pie type, Suzette also appeared to enjoy the "bad-boy" image of her tough ghetto-bred boyfriend. He seemed to stir in her feelings she had supressed in her very prim and proper middle-American existence. In the back of the limo, there were a lot of chicken-in-the-bucket dinners followed by wild sex.

Mike Tyson and Suzette Charles had a nice relationship which lasted all the way to the Desiree Washington incident a few years later. Don King, the infamous boxing-promoter with the electrified hair, had been circling Tyson like a buzzard since 1987, realizing back then that the only real heavyweight meal ticket in town had Mike Tyson's name written all over it. Tyson had been knocking out each and every one of Don King's boxers. As a small part of his master plan to win Tyson's affection and unquestioned loyalty, Don King hired Suzette Charles as a spokesperson for some of the fights he promoted. Once Tyson heard a rumor that King had been sleeping with her. He felt betrayed, but King, like he had so many other times, convinced Tyson the rumor was false.

MT loved to give expensive presents to his girlfriends, jewelry, designer clothes, sometimes even automobiles. At the same time, no matter how sincere they appeared to act toward him, Tyson still believed deep down that all women were really after his money instead of him. The more beautiful they were, the more insecurity they generated for him. It added enormous-ly to Tyson's insecurity to think they would be having sex with other men at the same time he was spending great sums of money on gifts for them. MT worried a lot about what his pretty women were doing when they weren't around him.

Although Tyson dated glamorous women who were in the news, he never stopped being with ordinary girls from his old neighborhood and others wherever he met them. MT seemed to be more at ease with rough-looking street girls than with celebrities. He was self-conscious about his lack of formal education and high-pitched, lisping voice. In almost every city we visited, we would pass through the red-light district, but only to watch the spectacle, never to reach out and touch someone. Occasionally, Tyson would have some fun with the hookers, rolling down the window so they could catch a glimpse of him. Once they recognized him, they would scream and run after us as we pulled away. One night we caused a small riot on 42nd Street in the City. As his window descended, Tyson called out to a group of ladies of the night.

"Hey, how can a brother get some ass around here?"

When the hookers realized who the potential client was, a huge army of pimps and hookers emerged from nowhere, flashing body parts, chasing us for the better part of two blocks. Tyson got a big laugh out of that scene.

I had seen Tyson with some beautiful white women, Vegas showgirls for example, but they never triggered jealousy in him. It only applied to black women. This was demonstrated to me very clearly in an incident which occurred in the spring of 1991. Tyson had a girlfriend from Los Angeles named Hope, very beautiful and very big tits. She had a tremendous sexual appetite. The three words Hope used most often were "yes" and "oh yes." She told me she wanted to sleep with me, but that would have been the end of my career with MT. If he suspected somebody on the staff or one of his friends was getting it on with one of his girls, they were out of Mike Tyson's life. He gave you just enough rope to hang yourself. I wasn't about to mess things

57

up. MT was still puzzled after all this time by not being able "to get anything" on me. When he sent me to get gas or do an errand, I returned right away. Tyson would tell me to take time off, but then I wouldn't go anywhere.

"You're always around," he would say, shaking his head.

Mike Tyson wasn't used to this type of loyalty. Too many people already had taken advantage of him during his rapid rise to fame and fortune. He would show his appreciation for my respect and loyalty by always giving me the customary hug. Sometimes the hug turned into a half-nelson, dragging me along as he kept on walking. No matter how busy MT was on any particular day, he always let me know he could count on me.

One night after Hope had visited MT in his LA apartment, he told me to follow her. She had left earlier than usual, telling him that she had to visit with a friend. He wanted me to find out where she went, if she made any calls, if she talked to anybody, if she met anybody, everything that she did after leaving him that night. So I grabbed the black Lamborghini Diablo and kept a discreet distance behind Hope's car. At Roscoe's, a soulfood hangout in downtown LA, she parked, got out of her car, and walked over to a black Lexus. After she spoke for a few moments with the driver, they went inside the restaurant. Her friend turned out to be actor Wesley Snipes.

MT was paging me. I called him back and let him know the situation. He told me to go see what was happening inside the restaurant. I told him that Hope was sitting on Snipes' lap. Once Tyson knew that Hope was "involved" with another guy, I suspected things were going to happen very quickly. Less than ten minutes later, he pulled up in the yellow Ferrari Testarossa, accompanied by our new body-guard, Anthony Pitts. Anthony was a former professional football player, stood about six-seven, and weighed in around two-fifty. Tyson jumped out of the Ferrari.

Anthony looked over at me. "There's gonna' be trouble."

We followed quickly behind MT. When Hope caught sight of him, she practically fell out of Snipes' lap onto the floor. The actor froze, then waved a hand: "Now, Mike, now, Mike, we can do this together. I don't want no problem."

"Let's go in the bathroom!" Tyson snapped. "Rudy, put Hope in the car."

When I returned from the parking lot, I noticed Anthony was blocking the bathroom door. A couple of minutes later we heard a big noise inside, and then Tyson emerged alone.

"Gimme' the keys to the Lamborghini," he mumbled.

After he was gone, I cracked open the bathroom door. Wesley Snipes was sitting on the floor against the far wall, head tilted to one side, unconscious.

At the opening of an Oprah Winfrey film called *The Women of Brewster's Place*, MT met an actress two years his senior named Robin Givens. Tyson had been given a cameo role, playing a tough guy with an eyepatch. Robin showed her continuing interest in him by spending some time with the champ in Vegas and attending his Pinklon Thomas fight which was held at the Hilton on May 30, 1987. After that fight, MT had two free months, until August 1, when he was to fight Tony Tucker for the IBF title. Much of those two months he spent with Robin.

As the year marched on there was no question that MT was more interested in Robin Givens than either Naomi Campbell or Suzette Charles. There was no future with Naomi. She represented one extreme. Naomi was completely independent, very wealthy and famous in her own right, unattainable, the pinnacle of all black women. Suzette was beautiful, polite, and caring, but her fifteen minutes of fame as a former Miss America were over.

Robin Givens presented herself at that time as the perfect compromise. She was a well-known black tv actress, but she was not a megastar. She was nice but also had a fiesty personality which made MT identify more easily with her than Suzette. And, of course, MT considered her to be one of the most beautiful black women he had ever set eyes on. After he had been with her for a few months, it was obvious he was deeply involved. He told me he couldn't believe somebody so beautiful wanted to be with him.

I met Robin Givens for the first time when MT sent me

to fetch her at the Philly airport and bring her to the Ocean Club. It was clear from the beginning that she wasn't thrilled MT's full-time chauffeur was a Puerto Rican. She outright told me she didn't like Spanish people because she claimed her father was Hispanic and had abandoned the family. There were to be no courtesies or "thank yous" from Robin Givens. I was just someone who opened doors for her. To me she was going to be a witch and a bitch from the start.

Before she married Mike Tyson, Robin Givens was a very proper tease. He was fascinated with her manner of virgin innocence. She also did a great "shy girl" act which made him feel in control, unlike when he was in the presence of super-self-confident Naomi Campbell.

"Did I kiss good, Mike?" she would ask him innocently.

I knew it was all a grand production, but it wasn't my place to interfere in MT's personal life. I heard she had been hanging out with Eddie Murphy, who I already knew was far from being a saint, and had developed a reputation as somewhat of a groupie in the tv business back in LA where she filmed *Head of the Class*.

At one point, Robin Givens believed she finally had conquered the undefeated champ. It was then that she let her guard down, showing some of her true stripes. When this happened, even though he continued to act like a fool in love when he was around her, Tyson resisted the idea of tying the knot. "She has wanted me to marry her for a long time but I ain't going to do it," he once said. "Hey, I'm only twenty-one, and I want to play the field for awhile. Besides, we fight all the

61

time. She thinks she is so much better than me, just because she's had an education. It may be true, but I hate the way she goes about telling me. I retaliate by telling her I am the heavyweight champion, and she should know her place. Man, she really gets into a temper at that and comes at me. She knows she can't hurt me if she kicks me in the head so she tries to kick me in the groin."

Robin Givens knew she had to pull out all the stops if she was going to land Mike Tyson. Early in February of 1988, aware of Camille Ewald's powerful influence over him, Givens called her up at The White House in Catskill, New York. Her goal was to get Tyson's eighty-three-year-old surrogate mother signed up with her program.

"She was upset about Mike and other girls," Camille related. "I told her: Mike is young. He's a champion. He doesn't know how to say no. He may see other girls, and he may let them kiss him, but that doesn't mean he goes to bed with them."

Givens responded: "I'm not one of his bimbos."

On January 22, 1988, Mike Tyson was scheduled to defend his three heavyweight belts against the challenger, Larry Holmes, at the Atlantic City Convention Center. He was looking for his thirty-third straight victory. In the fourth round, Holmes, a former champ, was knocked to the canvas three times before the referee intervened and stopped the fight. With yet another Tyson knockout victory, there was great celebration in the elegant ballroom of the Trump Plaza.

However, something very big had been brewing for a few weeks prior to the fight which radically would change Mike Tyson's life forever. I didn't know it at the time, but it was the beginning of the end. The whole process would take nearly four years to play out, but the wheels already had been set in motion during that cold month in January of 1988 when Robin Givens' mother, self-styled businesswoman Ruth Roper, informed Tyson co-managers Jim Jacobs and Bill Cayton that their fighter had gotten her daughter pregnant.

On February 8, I chauffeured MT and Robin to the home of a Catholic priest, Father George Clements, who married them that night. Tyson and Givens earlier had met the priest that evening at the NBA All-Star game in Chicago. At that time, we had a Mercedes 500SEL Carbriolet limousine with 18K gold rims. All the knobs and buttons inside the car and the exterior emblems were studded with diamonds. On February 9, Roper called Tyson's co-managers and warned them that if they didn't take steps to make the "religious ceremony" a legal marriage, then she would get the couple formally hitched in Nevada. The next day Tyson and Givens appeared at Manhattan's Municipal Building for a civil proceeding which legalized the union. On St. Valentine's Day, Tyson's new mother-in-law threw a ritzy party for an intimate group at the Helmsley Palace Hotel on Madison Avenue.

During this time, I wasn't with Tyson who had assigned Caesar and James Anderson to protect Robin. Tyson had dispatched me to Atlantic City to clean and organize the Ocean Club penthouse. Then I was to head to The White House to pick up the training team and check on Camille, who recently had undergone hip surgery. As soon as I arrived, Kevin Rooney and I discussed the news about the new Mrs. Tyson. Tyson had called Camille to inform her that she had a new daughter-in-law the morning after the religious ceremony in Father Clements' house. I had seen too many fights between the couple. I also knew that MT resented Givens' growing bossiness. Therefore, I was disappointed to find out that MT had chosen Givens as his first wife. Camille announced that the wedding party was going to continue at The White House.

When I reached the City, MT gave me the customary hug and asked how his mother was doing. He also wanted to know about his pigeons. Ever since he was a child, Tyson, like many ghetto kids, loved these birds. He kept more than two-hundred at The White House, including some which were very rare. I filled him in on the status of the penthouse apartment in Atlantic City and the other things I had been doing the past few days.

I immediately noticed the huge rock on Robin Givens' ring finger. Her wedding ring was the size of a golf ball. Tyson was wearing a simple wedding band. I chauffeured the newlyweds, Cayton, Rooney, Lott, and Rory Holloway back to the Catskills for the continuation of the wedding festivities. Cayton had bad chemistry with Holloway, one of Tyson's closest friends. Holloway had started hanging around all the time. For some reason Bill Cayton had a gut feeling that Holloway was going to be a bad influence on his fighter.

Tyson sat in the front with me all the way to The White House, listening to rap music. He appeared genuinely happy to be married. There was no doubt that he was very much in love with Robin Givens, even though their relationship over the past few months had turned from fairly tranquil to frequently argumentative. Mike Tyson had found the missing link in his life. He had amassed great fame and fortune in his professional boxing career. Now he was adding to it a permanent relationship with the girl of his dreams. And MT was very excited about two properties Givens had told him they should be considering to purchase as their main residence, one of which was the Vanderbilt mansion in Bernardsville, New Jersey. He also mentioned that he wanted to buy a Rolls Royce limousine, an idea enthusiastically embraced by his new wife.

During the ride up to the Catskills, MT patted me on the back. "You're doing a good job, Rudy."

I never tried to be Mike Tyson's friend or get involved in his private life. The idea that I should "know my place"

65

did not offend me. I was hired help, but I was very grateful for the opportunity to work for this champion, especially the more I learned about the Tyson tradition started by Cus D'Amato and the more people I met along the way who were part of it. Despite what I had seen and heard, I was determined to keep to myself my bad feelings about Robin Givens. If this relationship was going to survive, they needed all the support they could get. At all times I was very respectful of their privacy, hiding out in my room whenever they didn't need me to chauffeur them around, run errands, or provide security.

Events had moved too swiftly for co-managers Jim Jacobs and Bill Cayton, the people who carefully and fairly had managed Tyson's business affairs since he turned pro in 1985. There hadn't been time to discuss with their fighter the very important threshold matter of a prenuptial agreement. Perhaps Tyson had raced to the altar as a result of being tricked. Perhaps Robin Givens really wasn't pregnant. There were many unanswered questions, and they were going unanswered at one of the worst times for these two Tyson confidantes because they both were dealing with severe health problems. Cayton had been admitted to the hospital for inflammation of the heart membranes, and Jacobs had undergone intestinal surgery. Within days, their worst fears materialized. Ruth Roper, now taking charge of the business affairs of the newlyweds, demanded through an attorney that the co-managers immediately turn over every piece of paper relating to their handling of Mike Tyson.

Tyson really didn't know much, or even care to know much, about this fighting behind the scenes. We were in Japan preparing for the Tony Tubbs fight scheduled for March 21 at the Tokyo Dome. The newlyweds used part of this time to have the honeymoon they hadn't yet taken. They did a lot of sightseeing in limos furnished by companies promoting the Tyson-Tubbs fight, and they also provided security. I mostly tagged along with the security people.

Because I was doing very little chauffering during this period, Tyson assigned me additional duties as part of my daily responsibilities. I started placing calls for him, managing his appointment book, making arrangements for anything he needed, and providing security for him and Robin. It was during this trip to Japan that I became more than his chauffeur. I became his personal assistant and bodyguard as well. He knew from my prior service that I would get results quickly, professionally and courteously.

After awhile, the new Mrs. Tyson headed back to the States to immerse herself in finalizing the deal to purchase the Vanderbilt mansion located in Bernardsville, New Jersey. We later learned that there had been a big ruckus at the offices of Merrill Lynch because James Brady, Tyson's account executive, refused to turn over financial records to Givens without his customer's authorization. Givens returned to Japan a week before the fight followed by Don King who already was taking steps to get the Givens-Roper team in his corner.

What really was troubling Mike Tyson was the absence of Jim Jacobs who was lying in a bed in New York City's Mount Sinai Hospital. Jacobs had been battling leukemia for a number of years, and things weren't looking very good for him. Before Cus D'Amato died, he told Tyson that he should look to Jim Jacobs as the person to most trust in his absence. After D'Amato died, Jim Jacobs took over as Tyson's father figure, spending a great deal of time with him as counselor and friend.

When Tyson finally got in the ring with Tony Tubbs, these external pressures didn't appear to distract him. The champion, as he already had done so many times, made short work of his opponent. He wanted to perform better than ever, to get the match over with quickly, so he could attend to the pressing matters. It only took two rounds for Tyson to knock Tubbs out. The two persons closest to him were suffering, and he needed to give them his undivided attention. His wife was experiencing stomach pains and vomiting, probably related to complications of her pregnancy. And Tyson was eager to get back to New York so he could visit Jim Jacobs who remained hospitalized at Mount Sinai Hospital. Al Braverman, Don King Production's public- relations man, had spread a rumor that Jacobs had AIDS and had gone to Mexico for a treatment where he would receive a change of blood. Everybody was on the same 747 Japan Airlines flight back to the United States. Robin Givens and her mother were on board as well as Tyson's mother, Camille Ewald, and his "brother" from The White House, Jay Bright. There was co-manager Bill Cayton and his wife, Doris, as well as their family physician, cardiac-specialist Dr. Ira Gelb. Trainers Kevin Rooney and Steve Lott were there. And there was Don King who was entertaining anybody who cared to listen.

Cayton and Lott already were making plans for the much-publicized upcoming match with Michael Spinks scheduled for June 27 at Atlantic City's Convention Center. It wasn't long into the flight that Givens approached Cayton, requesting that he comply with her previous request to turn over the papers relating to his management of her husband. Cayton assured her that, once he was back at his office, she would get the documents she was seeking.

It was clear to me at that point, as I sat back to get some sleep on the Trans-Pacific flight, that 1988 was going to

69

be a very different type of year. The Tyson tradition started by Cus D'Amato back in 1979 looked like it was in for some very rocky times. Now, there were new kids on the block named Givens and Roper. And with Don King in the wings adding more fuel to the fire, it looked like there was going to be a lot of heat in the days to come.

Jim Jacobs died on March 23, 1988, the day after we landed at Kennedy Airport on our return trip from the Tony Tubbs fight at the Tokyo Dome. We all flew out to California to attend Jacobs' funeral in Culver City. The rabbi who conducted the service recalled the very interesting life of Tyson's co-manager. He had been a championship handball player, a light-heavyweight boxer, a master collector of baseball cards and professional boxing films, and a financial wizard. MT, a pallbearer, cried throughout the ordeal. Jacobs' death hit him harder than any boxing opponent could ever dream.

Robin Givens and her mother had no interest in attending the funeral of the most important man in Mike Tyson's life. Instead, they were determined to return to Merrill Lynch and again confront Jim Brady, Tyson's account executive. They expected things to be different this time. They produced a document giving Robin Givens authority over the account. There were angry shouts and accusations when they still didn't get the satisfaction they came looking for. They threatened to pull Tyson's money from Merrill Lynch and stormed out.

When we returned from the funeral in California, it appeared Tyson wasn't interested in getting in the middle of the rivalries which had sprung up after his marriage to Robin Givens. Still crushed by Jim Jacobs' death, he tried to divert his attention to their newly-acquired Bernardsville mansion. He was excited about getting the place ready for their first child and, hopefully, for several more down the road.

71

Tyson also worked at demonstrating his love for his wife, leaving gifts for her, diamonds under her pillow, roses on the nightstand. One time he took her breakfast in bed, having hidden a large diamond in her omelette. He was trying to do the right thing to make the marriage work. But Givens never seemed to be satisfied. She acted like she was owed these attentions and possessions, including the $4 million Bernardsville mansion. She also treated him like a dumb guy many times, usually failing to acknowledge his romantic efforts with even a kind word. Robin Givens' attitude was: "Is this all I'm getting?"

I would chauffeur her around to designer boutiques, Versace, Chanel, Gucci, Louis Vuitton, and other exclusive stores. She also could spend hours in Bloomingdales. If she saw something she liked in a showroom window, she would order me to pull over the limo so she could run inside and buy the item without thinking twice, no matter what it cost Mike Tyson. That's why I silently began to call her "Robin Gotta'-Have-It Givens." After their divorce, when I ventured telling my boss about the unofficial name I had given her, he had a good laugh.

The Bernardsville estate was about forty minutes from mid-town Manhattan. We usually would take the George Washington Bridge to get there. Whitney Houston had a residence next door. The mansion had twenty-five bedrooms and fourteen bathrooms spread among its three floors. Robin Givens took it upon herself to replace the decor originally styled by the Vanderbilt family. She spent more in renovations than it cost to purchase the residence. The main staircase and bannister were ripped out and redone in gold at a cost of around one-million.

The master bedroom was done in gold leaf, and the bathroom was bigger than most bedrooms. There was both a wet and dry sauna. And the shower had twenty jets at different angles and was so large it accommodated a set of cast iron furniture. The new Mrs. Tyson ordered a Roman-style marble tub, designed by Gianni Versace and encrusted with diamonds, which alone cost two million. This work was going on around the clock to get the place ready within a month.

At the same time, my boss was having me chauffeur him and his wife to Brownsville so she could get to know his roots. He would have me stop off at soul food places and Church's Fried Chicken. It was pretty easy to see that Mrs. Tyson wasn't particularly thrilled with these excursions back to Brooklyn to see "the home-boys." Her dislike of being reminded about her husband's roots would eventually blow up into a major conflagration in the not-too-distant future.

About the same time the Bernardsville mansion was

finished, the ten-pack Rolls Royce Silver Spur limousine was delivered. We had been using the grey fourteen-pack Mercedes with the raspberry interior. Now we had a Rolls just like in the old days when I chauffered Tyson around for Michelle's limo service. I had a special bag crafted so that we could keep track of all the keys to the vehicles in our inventory which now numbered around twenty-five.

Givens immediately took over as boss of the mansion's staff. Her quick temper and zero tolerance terrorized everybody. One time Givens told the chef to clean his jacket after she noticed it had a tomato sauce stain. He was busy cooking so he didn't do anything about it right away. Later, Givens saw that he hadn't yet followed her orders.

"Don't clean the jacket," she snapped. "Just take it off. You're fired."

Robin Givens fired a lot of people at the Bernardsville mansion. Tyson would try and hire some of them back, but many refused to return because Givens was an abusive employer. It wasn't long before there were signs of a storm on the horizon of this marriage. Givens still had her own career on track. She was involved in making films and also attended numerous social affairs. These commitments required that she be away from him for extended periods of time on the West Coast 3,000 miles away. When she returned to Bernardsville, he would want to know everything she had been doing. The times they were together at social gatherings, Givens was too friendly with other guys for MT's taste. He would fly into jealous rages, demanding to know why she had been looking at certain guys. Yet, Tyson later would feel guilty because he had been catting around while she was away from Bernardsville. He was still seeing Naomi Campbell and Suzette Charles on the side.

Although her belly didn't appear to expand during the spring of 1988, Robin Givens reportedly suffered a miscarriage in June. There would be no baby in Bernardsville in 1988. And so it was that, as the marriage entered its fourth month, Tyson restructured my duties. I now was "assigned" to his wife. This was to facilitate knowing where she was and what she was doing at all times he wasn't with her. For example, if she went shopping, he wanted to know if she was buying anything for a man. Tyson constantly would beep me, asking me what was going on. Givens didn't like the idea my being her husband's eyes and ears whenever she was out of his sight. The feeling was mutual.

At this time, two individuals, Rory Holloway and John Horne, were stoking the fires of discord between the couple. Holloway was a childhood friend from Brownsville who had moved to Albany and started hanging around Tyson all the time after his boxing career took off. Horne, who now lived in California, had known Holloway in Albany. Through Holloway in the spring of 1988, Horne wedged his way into Mike Tyson's life. The more Holloway and Horne whispered into Tyson's ear about his marriage, the more his jealous rages grew, even though I hadn't collected any dirt on his wife. It must have been his old insecurity stirring up inside now that the reality of his marriage finally was sinking in. Givens' spending sprees, the multi-million-dollar renovation of their home, the expensive clothing and jewelry, coupled with her manner of frequently talking down to him, must have made him conclude that she was no different than the rest, after his money, not him. With this in mind, the thought that his wife flirted with other men while she was away from him must have been unbearable.

One night when the jealousy really was getting to him, MT told me to take him into Manhattan. Tyson did the club scene, Bentley's, Nell's, and the Apollo Theater, guzzling down $400 champagne. He didn't drink that much because he didn't hold his liquor well. But that night he went on a bender and got plastered. Givens, who also developed the habit of constantly beeping me to find out what her husband was doing, tried dozens of times to get me to respond that night. MT told me not to respond.

Back at Bernardsville, I had to help him into the house. He was laughing and giggling uncontrollably. Waiting for us at the top of the elegant gold spiral staircase in her nightgown was Robin Givens.

"I'm only gonna' tell you this one time!" she shouted down at me. "You use the service entrance!"

Tyson looked over at me. "Who's she talking to?" Then he looked up at her. "Bitch, the only servant here is you."

He stumbled up the stairs after her, and she slammed the bedroom door and locked it before he reached her.

"Get away from me!" I heard her shouting.

Tyson kicked down the door and passed out. MT was no stranger to sleeping without the comfort of a bed. In all the time I worked for him, I never saw him sleep on one. He hated beds. Apparently it went back to a childhood trauma involving a bed. I had seen Tyson that first night in November of 1986 at JFK sleeping in a fetal position next to a ledge. Mike Tyson usually slept on the floor or, at best, half-on, half-off a couch. And he *never* had sex on a bed.

The pace of the fireworks between the two began picking up at the half-way point of the marriage. Although their sex life seemed good, they would have frequent arguments, sometimes ending with Tyson and Givens chasing each other down the New Jersey Turnpike. There was a lot of shoving and pushing, the majority of which was initiated by Givens. She didn't know how to stop with her mouth or hands. She was feisty. In the heat of battle, Robin would lunge at him and start scratching. I saw MT do his best to hold back. There was a good deal of yelling and screaming which included Ruth Roper, whose strategic position in the next bedroom allowed her to know what was going on between the couple. Tyson didn't want Roper in the house, but Robin insisted not only that her mother live with them but that she occupy the bedroom next door.

Not long after that there was another clash between MT and his wife which turned out to be their biggest ever. Tyson had planned a party for all his friends from the old Brownsville neighborhood. He wanted to give them the opportunity to have a good time for a full day away from the ghetto. He was expecting around two- hundred people. A company had been hired to make barbecue. In the morning the day of the party, a huge truck pulled up to the Bernardsville mansion. The truck opened up into a gigantic barbecue pit, and the caterers started preparing the big feast.

I was sitting around with MT and Anthony watching videos while waiting for the guests to arrive. As usual, we were watching Tyson favorites, "Tom and Jerry" and "Roadrunner" cartoons and karate flicks. Robin Givens was notably absent. She had taken off earlier in the day in her silver-grey Porsche for a shopping excursion in the City, hitting her favorite spots, Chanel, Gucci, Versace, Gautier's, and, of course, Bloomingdale's. We were advised that another big truck had pulled up in the driveway so we went to find out what was going on because we weren't expecting any more deliveries.

The driver asked us where we wanted him to put the portable toilets. The problem was we hadn't ordered any. I could see Tyson's facial muscles twitching with anger.

"Rudy, call that bitch up and ask her why we have this truck here."

I raised Givens on her cellular. "Robin, the boss wanted me to ask you if you ordered some portable toilets for the party."

She preferred I called her by her first name rather than "Mrs. Tyson."

"Yes, I ordered the toilets. I don't want any of those nasty niggers from Brooklyn using my bathrooms."

I turned to MT. "Yes, sir, she said she doesn't want those nasty niggers using..."

"Tell her to get her ass home now!"

Tyson was embarrassed and angry that his wife didn't think his friends from the old neighborhood were good enough to use the bathrooms of their home. His wife had overstepped one boundary she could never cross, no matter how much he was in love with her. He never lost sight of who he was or where he came from. He ordered the portable toilets be taken away. Later, Givens zoomed into the driveway and made her way to the tv room where we all were sitting.

"What's the problem?" she snapped.

Tyson jumped up and grabbed her by the neck. The rest of us also jumped up and pleaded with him to release her.

"Who are you to call my friends nasty niggers?" he yelled and kicked her in the ass. "Go to your room!"

Ten minutes later Ruth Roper descended the stairway and confronted Tyson. By that time, MT already was sick of Roper always correcting his manners and behavior toward her daughter. A shouting match broke out.

"She thinks she's white. She's as black as anything around here!"

There was no way he was going to apologize for his behavior. It was almost noon, and he turned to me.

"I want a favor. I want you to make as many trips to Brooklyn as it takes. Pick up everybody. And, Rudy, treat everybody the same."

The humble folks back in Brownsville had one hell of a time. I made seven round trips that day, picking up Tyson's guests at the housing projects. They were being chauffeured to Bernardsville in a Rolls Royce limousine, their driver a very sharply-dressed young man who made them feel like royalty. Tyson had spent a lot of money on my clothing. I was the only chauffeur I knew who wore leather clothing and alligator shoes. MT believed that if his chauffeur looked like a million bucks, then he would look like a billion sitting in the back of the limo.

I remember picking up one guy, William Fagan, who looked like he had been working under a car for three weeks, so dirty and greasy that he surely was going to mess up the limo. But I told him not to worry, to get in, that we would take care of him. We stopped off at a store on the way, and I bought him a sweatsuit and sneakers. I didn't know at the time that he was one of Tyson's most intimate childhood friends. Apparently, word got back to my boss about how well I had treated this guest. In fact, Tyson was told by many that I had been extremely polite and helpful to his guests. I didn't know that one of the passengers was his aunt. She had a problem walking, and I had helped her down the stairs from her apartment. One reason Tyson kept me in his service longer than anybody else was because I always made it a point to treat everybody courteously.

"Rudy, don't judge people because we're all the same," he would say. "Don't let the money change you."

The barbecue was a big success. After I had brought the last load of guests from his old neighborhood, MT walked over to me with a plate of chicken and ribs.

"Hey, take a break," he said, handing me the plate.

"You've been driving my people around all day. Let's have dinner together."

He told me that everybody was bragging about how great his chauffeur had treated them. This was the first time MT pulled me out of the role of chauffeur and personal assistant and consulted me like a friend, leaving his guests behind to have dinner with me.

After we had wolfed down the delicious barbecue, he said. "That Robin. I can't believe she'd do this to me. I don't understand why she is so selfish and greedy. She doesn't want my people to use our toilets. Even if they broke them all, I've got enough money to rebuild them tomorrow."

Rather than fuel the fire, I decided to throw water on it. "Robin is like that because she's just trying to protect your investments. There's a lot of stuff that could get broken."

"She's more worried about my people stealing the diamonds from the tubs. Why did the bitch order those tubs anyway? She never takes a bath in them."

He waved his arm around showing the expanse of the estate. "Don't let this shit get to you. We're just regular people."

Back then, it was easy to see that Mike Tyson cared about all types of people. Cus D'Amato and Camille Ewald, the two people who rescued him from the Tryon School reformatory and raised him as their own son, were white. Jim Jacobs, his co-manager, who took over as his father figure after Cus died was Jewish. Tyson picked me, a Puerto Rican, as his first and only full-time chauffeur who later became his personal assistant. Back then, Mike Tyson had friends from all colors, races, and religions. He couldn't be prejudiced because his personal experience had taught him that racism was, if anything, just plain foolish. But things were about to happen which would break Mike Tyson down and lead him astray, so much so, that he turned his back on these experiences and friendships that had pulled him from the ghetto and made him a world-champion boxer.

After the big barbecue with Mike Tyson's old friends from Brooklyn, the marriage between the couple began to unravel. In September, Robin Givens was scheduled to go to the Soviet Union because her tv sitcom, *Head of the Class*, was going to do two weeks of location shooting in Moscow. Tyson decided he also should go. And, as she did most of the time, his mother-in-law, Ruth Roper, also would accompany her daughter.

Approximately one month later, when Givens filed for divorce in Los Angeles, she stated in her petition that, among other things, Tyson had been out of control during the Moscow trip. She claimed that he had thrown champagne bottles around their hotel room. She also claimed that one time he visited the hotel bar, drank glass after glass of vodka like it was water, then returned to their room, gulped down a handful of lithium pills, and threatened to commit suicide. Then he threatened to kill Robin and her mother and chased them down to the lobby. When a Russian police officer tried to intervene, Tyson threatened him. She also stated that her husband "hung from the hotel balcony for about ten minutes, saying he was going to kill himself." Finally, she declared that Tyson kept chasing them "from about 1 a.m. until about 5 a.m." and "only stopped because we had to catch a plane." All of these allegations were unadulterated bullshit.

"We had no incidents whatsoever while he was here," Anatoli Mikheyev told the media. He was the house detective at the Rossiya hotel where the cast from the show stayed. "And if we had, I would have heard about them."

Head of the Class co-creator and co-executive producer Michael Elias stated that Tyson had shown up on the set but "was exemplary at all times. I never heard him raise his voice to anyone."

The truth was that the couple stayed at the Moscow Hilton, and there was one incident. Givens had appeared a little too friendly with some of the men whom she encountered in the lobby. Tyson grabbed her harshly, shook her, and in a loud voice made known his feelings about her behavior. That was the extent of any "violence."

During the trip to the Soviet Union, Givens and her mother wanted to acquire expensive Russian furs. Tyson bought six coats while we were there, including a rare black sable which cost around $300,000. To pay for them, Tyson contacted Bill Cayton back in New York and had him wire funds. Apparently Roper's appetite for furs wasn't yet satisfied. Just a few days after we returned from the Soviet Union, Roper had her son-in-law buy her a golden sable coat with a price tag of more than $90,000.

That very same evening, Givens and Roper appeared on ABC's "*20/20*." A few days before in Los Angeles, Givens had told MT that Barbara Walters wanted to swing by the house and do an interview. She was kissing and smooching him, and he said "okay, whatever." The night they taped the interview, Givens and Roper told Walters that Mike Tyson was a "sick, sick man," a violent manic-depressive, and that their life with this "beast" was "pure hell." MT also was on camera, sitting meekly by them as they pummelled him with these false and vicious accusations. The show was broadcast to millions across the nation. I learned later that Camille Ewald and Jay Bright had watched the show together at The White House and had become outraged at this humiliating spectacle.

Although Givens and Roper had sent him to a psychiatrist who prescribed anti-psychotic, mood-altering drugs for him, there was nothing wrong with Mike Tyson. After Givens filed for divorce, he was examined by a very well-respected psychiatrist, Dr. Abraham L. Halpern, chairman of the Department of Psychiatry at United Hospital in Port Chester, New York. Dr. Halpern did a thorough exam of Tyson as well as background interviews with friends and family. He concluded that Mike Tyson was "free of any signs of psychotic thinking or behavior. He showed no manifestations of manic-depressive illness, nor did I find any basis to believe that he had, in the past, exhibited symptoms of manic-depressive psychosis or manic-depressive illness." Dr. Halpern checked out his findings with Dr. Henry McCurtis, the psychiatrist to whom Givens and Roper had sent Tyson. Dr. McCurtis agreed that the fighter didn't suffer from any mental condition, contrary to what Givens and Roper had broadcast to millions on "20/20."

On October 7, 1988, one week after Roper had received her $90,000 golden sable coat, Marvin Mitchelson, the flamboyant palimony lawyer, told the world he was representing Robin Givens and had filed divorce papers on her behalf in Los Angeles. Because the action was filed in California, a community-property state, Givens would be seeking one-half of everything her husband had earned since the moment they were married, even though the marriage had survived for only eight months. This was in contrast to the law in other states, such as New York or New Jersey, where marriages were reviewed on a case-by-case basis to reach fair and equitable divisions of the parties' marital assets.

At a press conference Mitchelson said: "Should she be treated differently because they were married a short period of time? If there were two dollars in this case, they'd each be entitled to a dollar."

At this time, Mike Tyson stopped using the anti-psychotic drugs lithium and Thorazine. In a New Jersey court he filed a petition for annulment or, alternatively, divorce, asserting that Givens tricked him into the marriage by making up a story about being pregnant. It wouldn't have been the first time Givens had been caught telling a falsehood. The *New York Daily News* had published an article, claiming that Givens had lied on her resume about several accomplishments, acceptance into Harvard Medical School, studies at the American Academy, and being a "top young model" at New York's prestigious Ford Agency.

That same day he filed his own papers in the New Jersey court, Tyson was interviewed by the *Chicago Sun-Times*.

"This issue is not money," he said. "It's just the idea that they played a scheme on me. They drew me in, they worked on my emotions because I was in love. They tried to separate me from my friends."

In his written pleadings in the California proceedings, Tyson stated that he had "been tricked into marriage" and was "the hapless victim of intentional fraud."

I wasn't surprised by the torrent of false accusations and humiliation which had rained down on MT at the end of this marriage. Although not as easy to detect at the beginning of the relationship, as time passed it was clear to me that Givens and Roper didn't care at all about Mike Tyson, only his money. They saw this marriage as a business proposition, spending more hours discussing Mike Tyson's career with each other than MT did working out in the gym.

Muhammed Ali had several favorite phrases to describe how he tricked and suckered his opponents into defeat. One of those was the "ropa-dopa." I thought how ironic it was that Mike Tyson's mother-in-law was named Ruth Roper because, during his short and rocky relationship with Roper and her daughter, he got "Roper-doped." Tyson ended up settling the divorce litigation with Givens. After eight months as Mrs. Tyson, Robin Givens walked out of his life for good, millions richer in property and cash.

On more than one occasion when he wasn't around, I had heard Roper and Givens refer to my boss' favorite dog, a bull mastiff, as "Mike Tyson."

"Bait and Switch"

After doing four years in Ohio's Marion Correctional Institution for murdering a business associate, Don King, the ex-numbers runner from Cleveland, turned to a career of promoting professional boxing. By the mid-eighties, he had added a new credit to his resume, "world's premier fight promoter." And he had made tons of money as he reached the summit of his profession, handling such world champions as Muhammed Ali and Larry Holmes.

But by mid-1986, Don King started experiencing a run of very bad luck. His heavyweight fighters were being knocked out right and left by a young black teenager from Brownsville with an eccentric past, having been raised in the Catskills since age twelve by boxing legend Cus D'Amato and his companion, Camille Ewald. By July of 1986, Michael Gerard Tyson had won all of his twenty-five professional fights, twenty-three by knockouts, and that had been in less than eighteen months. Because Mike Tyson was only twenty years old, the writing on the wall jumped out at Don King: Mike Tyson was going to be somebody's major meal ticket for years to come.

This was made clearer to Don King when he was arranging "The Heavyweight Unification Tournament" with another promoter, Butch Lewis. King had dubbed himself and Lewis as "The Dynamic Duo." The Tournament was being co-promoted by the Las Vegas Hilton Hotel and Home Box Office, the idea being at the end of the Tournament to have a single heavyweight champion of the world. Presently, there was no such "undisputed" champion due to the existence of three major organizations, the WBC, WBA, and IBF, each of which sponsored professional boxing matches. However, things weren't spinning out very well for Don King and his project. Advance sales on the fight between Michael Spinks and Norwegian Steffen Tangstad were so minimal as to spell financial disaster for the much-hyped Unification Tournament.

In desperation and to the surprise of many, Don King agreed to bring into the fold the Tyson fight scheduled for September 6, 1986 against Alfonso Ratliff. He did this reluctantly because his cut wasn't going to be very favorable, only a fixed fee rather than his customary promoter's percentage. But the strategy saved the Heavyweight Unification Tournament, sales immediately skyrocketing once the young Tyson's name appeared on the Unification Tournament card. Tyson's Tournament opponents, Alfonso Ratliff, Trevor Berbick, "Bonecrusher" Smith, and Pinklon Thomas, all were controlled by Don King through exclusive contracts with him or through his son Carl. And Tyson had made them all fall like dominos. Don King was determined, either then or very soon thereafter, that he would take whatever steps were necessary to secure the lion's share of Mike Tyson's steamroller career. With the advent of cable tv and, on the horizon, pay-per-view, there just were too many millions to be made to not have this prize, especially if you were the "world's premier promoter."

But it was easier said than done. The Tyson tradition remained solid, even after Cus D'Amato died on November 4, 1985. First, Mike Tyson still had a home at The White

House in Catskill, New York, where he lived with the elderly Camille Ewald and the rest of his adoptive family. Second, his professional boxing career and growing wealth continued to be co-managed fairly and conservatively by long-time D'Amato intimate, Jim Jacobs, and his partner Bill Cayton, a successful entrepreneur. Third, the original crew, Kevin Rooney, Steve Lott, and Matt Baransky, were still training the fighter with the time-tested training techniques of Cus D'Amato. These were the very strong forces and influences on Mike Tyson's life from which he would not be lured away easily. Don King knew it would take extraordinary events and major upheavals in Mike Tyson's life before he could hope to break that tradition.

Don King got to work right away, checking the back door to see if it was open, even if only so slightly. As things got serious between Tyson and Robin Givens, King realized that the way to get to the young fighter was through the tv actress. And because Givens was in partnership with Ruth Roper, her mother also had to be included in the program. King began courting them and bombarding them with the party line: the white man still enslaved the black man, especially in the world of professional sports. It wasn't long before Givens and Roper began chipping away at Tyson's faith in those who had been around him for years. Givens and Roper tried to convince Tyson that his white management team didn't have his best interests at heart, and that there were major discrepancies in his financial records. Their theme song, promoted by Don King with as much pomp and circumstance as he did professional boxing, was simple. The white man has tricked you and violated your trust. He has been stealing your money. It's time to get rid of him and return to your people.

Within a few weeks after the couple married, Jim Jacobs passed away. With the opposition minus its quarterback, Roper and Givens stopped chipping and started hammering. They confronted Cayton periodically, demanding that he fade into the background while they took over more and more of Tyson's business affairs. Meanwhile, Cayton desperately was searching for ways to fight them off and ensure Mike Tyson's continued career development and financial security.

Givens and Roper were working for Don King and didn't even realize it. They thought landing Mike Tyson would be for their exclusive use and benefit. But King was miles ahead of them. Givens and Roper simply were used as stepping stones in the master game plan that was unfolding.

Don King had been working various angles for some time in his quest to win over Mike Tyson's affections. There had been the hooplah angle, throwing a corny "coronation" ceremony for Tyson after he won the Heavyweight Unification Tournament on August 1, 1987. Tyson was given a jeweled scepter from Felix the Jeweler, cloaked in a chinchilla robe from Lenobel Furriers, and topped with a jeweled crown which King described as studded with "baubles, rubies, and fabulous doodads." Tyson hadn't been impressed. In fact, he had resisted attending the silly spectacle. There had been the caring and concern angle when King flew to

California to console Tyson at Jim Jacobs' funeral.

Don King was very smart. He had that very special talent of being able to see the "big picture." He always saw the forest as well as the trees. Had he desired, Don King might have become a world-champion chess player. To increase the possibility of winning over Mike Tyson, Don King didn't want to be the first to risk alienating the strong bonds between Tyson and his extended family. He left that task to his own unwitting "dynamic duo," Robin Givens and Ruth Roper.

There was one obstacle which Don King hadn't anticipated as the Tyson marriage travelled down its rocky but still intact road into mid-1988. A very big factor had been looming in the wings but now was definitely coming into the picture. Donald Trump was at the summit of fame and power. Atlantic City was booming, and its star was the larger-than-life New York developer known as "The Donald." The Taj Mahal, a huge palace casino, was the crowning jewel of his many well-known properties.

Donald Trump had been involved with HBO for some time putting together professional boxing matches in Atlantic City. Several had Mike Tyson on the heavyweight card, Tyrell Biggs on October 16, 1987, and in 1988, Larry Holmes on January 22 and Michael Spinks on June 27. The very powerful Donald Trump was getting too involved in the world of professional boxing for Don King's taste. And in that world, Mike Tyson was the biggest game in town. Robin Givens connected Tyson with the Trumps. She had been palling around with Ivana Trump for awhile. The Trumps became very chummy with the Tysons, eventually inviting them to spend an extended period of time on their 225' yacht, the *Trump Princess* which was tied up behind the Trump Regent Hotel.

Don King began searching for a wrench to throw into that disturbing Trump-Tyson friendship. And because he always saw the big picture, King also was looking for a way to eventually dump Givens and her mother. And what better weapon to employ for these tasks than the services of Mike Tyson's closest friends. He found those friends in Rory Holloway and John Horne.

Bill Cayton had been keeping a wary eye on Holloway for some time. From the beginning, the training team and Tyson's co-managers made it clear to me that they believed Holloway was a bad influence and threat to their fighter's career. They knew Holloway took Tyson out for late night forays into the club scene. They also knew that Holloway ran with a bad crowd back in Albany. There wasn't much I could do except try and keep my boss out of trouble.

Tyson enjoyed visiting Holloway in Albany, and I must have taken him there several dozen times during the first two years I worked for him. I suspected that my boss liked the escape factor. When life's stresses got to him, Tyson liked to hit the road to upstate New York. Although his parents owned a small grocery store, Holloway wasn't doing much of anything when I met him. Tyson helped him out financially, sending him a weekly "paycheck." With this money, and by living with his parents, Rory Holloway drove a brand-new automobile and sported a Rolex watch. However, in the very near future, another source of funds would make Rory Holloway an overnight millionaire.

Like Robin Givens, Rory and I didn't get along very well either. Again, the feeling was mutual. Once, during May of 1988, MT wanted to fly out to Los Angeles to track down his wife. She was supposed to have returned to Bernardsville two days before after completing a shoot for *Head of the Class*. The studio hadn't been able to locate her, and MT was furious. Holloway already was in Los Angeles at the time and suggested he and Tyson hook up. I was chauffering them around in a rental limo which we had picked up at the airport. Holloway suggested that we head for The Comedy Club. When we arrived, MT told me to park the limo and come inside with them.

"Don't let that nigger come with us," Holloway protested. "What're you still doing with that stringy-haired motherfucker anyway? With all the niggers out there without a job, why you keep hanging around with that fool?"

Tyson got pissed at his friend. "Rory, don't tell me what to do! Rudy's been with me for a long time. Leave him alone."

Inside, as usual, I stood near MT, keeping an eye on things so he wouldn't be hassled. A tall, skinny black guy named John Horne came on stage to perform. He reminded me of Jimmy Walker from the tv comedy *Good Times* but, unlike Walker, Horne wasn't funny. Rory Holloway knew Horne from back in Albany, and Horne later had relocated to California. Although Holloway appeared "surprised" to run into his old friend at The Comedy Club, it was likely that Holloway already knew Horne would be there that night.

After his performance, Horne "realized" Holloway was at a table with Mike Tyson and hurried over.

"Hey, man!" he said, slapping Holloway's back, "What're you doing with Mike Tyson!"

They bullshitted for awhile, catching up on things. I could see the dollar signs flashing in Horne's eyes as he kept staring that evening at Tyson's gold jewelry and diamond Rolex watch. After awhile, Tyson was able to locate Givens, and we headed for a restaurant where she was waiting for him.   Everything turned out very lovey-dovey that night between MT and his wife.

Tyson wanted to drive with his wife cross-country back to New Jersey. He had a black Ferrari Testarossa which had been sitting in an LA parking lot for months. As a married man, with his life now centralized in Bernardsville, he wanted to bring all his important possessions to the estate. Givens didn't like the idea of a long drive so Tyson told me to bring the Testarossa. Over a period of four days, I got a lot of curious and envious stares whenever I pulled in to fill up for gas along I-70.

One morning not long after that, Tyson was eating his daily bowl of Captain Crunch. The chef could be whipping up shrimp or lobster omelettes, but Tyson wouldn't even look at them until he first had his ritualistic bowl of "CK" without milk. MT mentioned that he would be driving into the City with Givens for the day and for me to just hang out at the Bernardsville estate. Soon after they departed, I got a page from Rory Holloway.

"Yo, Rudy, I need you to do me a personal favor. I want you to pick up a friend of mine and bring him to my place."

"Yeah, who is it?"

Holloway told me it was John Horne, and I thought to myself, "oh, yeah, the comedian who's not funny." I knew Tyson would have wanted me to accomodate his close friend, so I agreed and left a note telling MT where I had gone. Holloway gave me instructions to go to Kennedy Airport. Horne was waiting for me, standing by the curb dressed in old jeans, sneakers, an LA Raiders t-shirt, and carrying a small duffel bag. When I pulled up in the $400,000 limousine, Horne's eyes bugged out. He literally was sniffing the rich leather seats during the drive to Albany.

After a four-hour drive, we pulled into the driveway of Rory Holloway's house. Holloway came out to greet us, hugging his buddy from California.

"Don't leave, Rudy. Give me a few minutes."

I was feeling anxious waiting around for these two after the long drive to Albany, especially because it was going to take me another four hours to return to Jersey. Tyson could reach me anytime through the Skypager, but I didn't like the idea of being pulled away from my regular duties. Finally, Holloway and Horne emerged from the house and jumped into the back of the limo.

"Take us to New York," said Holloway. "32 East 69th Street in Manhattan. And step on it. I need to get there fast."

I wasn't very happy about being told to make this additional trip, delaying further my return to Bernardsville.

"This is two tons of very expensive steel. I'll do my best."

"Just step on it, Rudy," Holloway said coldly.

MT didn't like reaching for buttons so he had installed a voice-activated intercom in his sound-proofed Rolls Royce limousine. Holloway and Horne didn't know about the system so I decided to get some revenge by eavesdropping on these two. They kept babbling excitedly about their meeting in the City, but I couldn't determine what it was about. They kept repeating that they "had to make it work."

We only stopped once during the trip, a rest stop on

the highway, where my passengers grabbed some food at McDonald's. Then it was on to 32 East 69th Street between Madison and Park Avenues. We pulled up to a beautiful brownstone with two huge flags in front, one the stars and stripes, the other a crown with the name "Don." I realized we had arrived at the offices of Don King Productions. Holloway told me to wait for them outside, and he and Horne entered the building. A few moments later a Rolls Royce sedan pulled up behind me. Don King, dressed in jeans and leather jacket, got out, his signature hair at attention, carrying a briefcase.

I waited there for three hours and watched the sun go down. I had been calling the mansion in Bernardsville repeatedly, but there was no answer. Because the estate was only forty minutes away, I was upset but not nervous as I was waiting around in upstate New York at Holloway's house.

I'll never forget the wide grins which Holloway and Horne were wearing when they finally descended the steps of Don King Productions. They piled into the limo, asked me to take them back to Albany, and quickly raised up the partition separating us. Now I was really pissed. I was looking at eight hours roundtrip before I would be back at Bernardsville. I thought about clearing this return trip first with MT. While I was considering what to do, I decided to again eavesdrop on my passengers by way of the voice-activated intercom.

"You believe that we just made the biggest deal in boxing history!" Horne was screaming. "We made it so fast and easy! Can you believe the nigger gave us one million in cash just to get the nigger to the table?" Horne kept squealing like an excited pig. "I can't believe it! I can't believe it!"

Holloway lowered the partition. "Where's Mike?"

When I told him that he probably was back in Jersey after a day of shopping in the City with Givens, Holloway ordered me to forget Albany and take them straight to Bernardsville. Then Holloway grabbed the phone in back and started trying to reach Tyson at the mansion. We arrived just as Tyson and Givens were unloading a large number of bags and packages.

Holloway ran over to MT. "Mike, Mike, we did it, we did it!" he said excitedly. They started walking toward the limo, Holloway hugging him and whispering in his ear.

"Mike, Mike!" Horne yelled, waving wildly at Tyson from inside the limo.

John Horne didn't know Mike Tyson at all, yet he was acting like he was an old friend. Horne noticed my expression.

"What are you looking at?"

"Nothing," I said. "What's the matter?"

Horne raised the partition as MT and Holloway approached.

"Why are you staying in the car?" Tyson asked me.

"Sir, there's somebody still inside."

"Who the fuck's in my limo?"

"It's John Horne, my boy from LA," Holloway beamed, shepherding Tyson into the back of the Rolls. "Take us to 221 East 62nd Street," he said.

I turned around to see what MT wanted me to do.

"Rudy, just drive the fucking car," Holloway snapped, raising the partition.

Because I didn't hear anything else, I started the limo and pulled out of the Bernardsville estate, heading toward Manhattan, noticing that Tyson had turned off the voice-activated intercom.

At 62nd Street between Second and Third Avenues, we pulled up to a striking four-story brownstone building with several security cameras. To my surprise, Don King opened the door. My passengers went inside while I waited for them to return. At about 10 p.m., I was standing next to the Rolls when a taxi pulled up behind me. Two men in suits carrying briefcases got out. They climbed the stairs to the front door and rang the bell. In a few moments, Don King answered and ushered them inside.

I don't know why but Don King glared over at me, with a look that gave me the chills, and then slammed the door. I had a feeling at that moment that there was something really wrong going on inside. Four hours later my three passengers left Don King's residence, and we headed back to Bernardsville. After that night, and until close to the end, Rory Holloway and John Horne stuck to Mike Tyson like he was their personal life-support equipment.

John Horne never returned to live in LA after that day I had picked him up at Kennedy Airport. He and Rory Holloway stayed in an apartment nearby and also with MT many times as houseguests. Whenever possible, they would hang out with MT until late into the night, then seek him out early the next morning. There was a very noticeable change in the conversations I started hearing on a daily basis around the Bernardsville mansion. Now it seemed like everything was a racial issue. Holloway and Horne began continuously pounding Mike Tyson with a "black rap." The white man, Bill Cayton, was using him and stealing his money. And his white trainers, Rooney, Lott, Baransky, didn't give the champion the same respect they would give to a white fighter. Instead, they treated him like a child and kept him on a very tight leash.

Holloway and Horne began cranking up another "rap" to lay on Mike Tyson. They started working to destroy his relationship with his tv actress wife. It wasn't clear at that time that their marriage would fail. The Tysons had become close to the Trumps, and MT seemed to enjoy this friendship, spending a good deal of time on the *Trump Princess* anchored at the marina. The more friends they shared, the better chance their marriage would have to survive. But Holloway and Horne were trying to get Tyson in a certain frame of mind: Robin Givens is taking your money while she's out sucking somebody else's dick.

These campaigns represented two very big gambles for Rory Holloway and John Horne. There had been, and still were, many white people intimately woven into Mike Tyson's human experience. Nobody had been more important to him than Cus D'Amato, except perhaps his own mother, Lorna, and his sister, Denise. And Tyson had great love for his adoptive mother, Camille Ewald, and great affection for his "brother" Jay Bright. Despite his fame and fortune, he had never turned his back on The White House in Catskill, New York. It was still his home, and the attic bedroom was still his bedroom, where he had many fond memories, where he spent hundreds of hours watching Jim Jacobs' collection of boxing films.

Even though the training team, Kevin Rooney, Steve Lott, and Matt Baransky, whom D'Amato had assembled to propel Mike Tyson to the summit of professional boxing, was very strict with him, he knew they cared about his welfare in every respect. Tyson had become very close to co-manager Jim Jacobs, a man who spent many hours counseling him after D'Amato's death. Although Tyson never developed that closeness with Bill Cayton, he was grateful to both of his co-managers for their careful and conservative management of his business affairs. And, of course, Mike Tyson was very much in love with Robin Givens, the girl of this young man's dreams, once believed beyond his reach, now permanently at his side.

But there was a method to the madness, this very big gamble by Rory Holloway and John Horne. And the method had been designed and patented by Don King.

Rory Holloway and John Horne were taking over so much by the early summer that they now ordered me to chauffeur them around. At the same time, there was a new and frequent visitor to the Bernardsville estate, Don King. Bill Cayton, aging and ailing, didn't know about this transformation in Mike Tyson's life.

Holloway and Horne used Givens' criticisms of Tyson's eating habits to their advantage, making fun of him for letting the bitch talk down to him. They also were aware that in front of him Givens would savor sumptuous meals prepared by the gourmet chef while he was relegated to the greaseless, tasteless foods prescribed for him while he was training. Kevin Rooney worked closely with the chef, ensuring that Tyson's caloric intake was carefully monitored. Tyson usually got very small portions of meats and vegetables, mostly turkey and carrots. It was no wonder MT wolfed down his food like an animal. He was always starving.

"Is this all you're getting?" I used to ask him at the beginning before I understood the dynamics of the training diet for a heavyweight fighter like Tyson.

"I know, shit! Can you fucking believe this Rudy?"

That's why he needed his Captain Crunch every day. His "CK" made him feel full, and his trainers wouldn't bother him about it, so he consumed it dry by the boxful.

One day, while Robin Givens was in Los Angeles filming *Head of the Class*, MT and I were driving around when he asked me to call Holloway on the cellular so they could catch a movie together. Holloway said he would meet Tyson at Victor's Cafe, a Cuban restaurant in Manhattan. I waited outside while Holloway and Horne sat with MT and had lunch. I could see them through the window, and they were laughing a lot. After awhile, they piled into the limo.

"You know, that bitch's doing you wrong, MT," Rory said. "She's sleeping around. Why you need her?"

"But I love her."

I could hear Holloway and Horne giggling and making fun of his response. They told him he was a fool, that she had to be sucking somebody else's dick because that was the reality of Hollywood. I had been noticing an evolution in MT's attitude ever since Holloway and Horne had been sticking to him like superglue. He was paying a lot more attention to their comments. Once they knew they had his ear, their comments about Robin Givens got increasingly vulgar. Tyson had assigned me to stay with Givens as much as possible, but I had never seen her flirting with anybody else or doing anything to raise my suspicions. As Holloway and Horne were well aware, if somebody tells you something *over and over* enough times, you're *eventually going to believe it.* That's the method used by all successful tyrants. Later I would learn that Don King, an enthusiastic student of the Nazi movement, particularly the propaganda techniques employed by Josef Goebbels, was the real force behind Horne and Holloway's constant bombardment of Tyson with these "raps."

It wasn't long before Horne and Holloway pulled out all the stops to make Tyson a single man again. They orchestrated things so that there always would be a lot of women

104

hanging around whenever Robin Givens was out of town. And Ruth Roper was in the dark because she went everywhere with her daughter. So there came a point in time when Tyson "groupies" were just about anywhere Holloway and Horne could get away with it, if not in Bernardsville, then at least in the privacy of the limousine. While Holloway had Tyson on a nostalgia trip, back to their wild days in the Albany club scene, Horne became responsible for organizing group sex.

During the last three months of their marriage, things rapidly went downhill between the Tysons. There were times when Robin called the Bernardsville mansion from the set of *Head of the Class* and heard music blasting and girls screaming in the background. Givens would rant and rave to her husband about his wild partying while she was out of town. But after enough megadoses of the "rap" laid on MT by Horne and Holloway, his response to Robin Givens became standard: "I don't give a shit. I'll do what I want."

By the end of the summer of 1988, Don King's master game plan, instead of being a very big gamble, started looking like a sure thing. For several months, two forces independently had been hard at work to achieve one of King's goals, the elimination of the Tyson tradition. First, Givens and Roper had been wearing down Mike Tyson with their "rap" about white people controlling his career and money, and they in fact already had secured certain concession from Cayton. Second, Holloway and Horne followed them, incessantly bombarding Tyson with the same "rap."

Not long after Robin Givens had humiliated Mike Tyson and announced in Los Angeles that she was filing for divorce, he fired Kevin Rooney, the man whom Cus D'Amato hand-picked to oversee his training. Rooney tirelessly had worked to take the fighter to the top of his profession and also had tried to be a good friend along the way. In late November of 1988, Tyson had seen Rooney on tv where the trainer gave the impression that having Don King to deal with was going to be worse than Givens. The next day, Kevin Rooney, who didn't have a written contract, who had worked for years on the strength of a handshake, was out. Steve Lott, the second trainer, had been fired sometime before. And an official battle had broken out between Cayton and King, who was promoting Tyson fights without authority from Cayton. He was just doing it. Pieces of the Tyson tradition, a solid rock for a number of years, were falling to the ground.

Mike Tyson never mentioned to me that he was going to fire Kevin Rooney or anybody else. Whether he made these decisions or simply just communicated them, I really don't know. By this stage, his mind was so messed up by all the negative forces working around him that he "just didn't want to know anything." For a time he had been refusing to take calls from Rooney, Lott, and Cayton, the people upon whom he most needed to rely to protect his best interests. But he was too busy with his new life filled with intrigue provided by Rory Holloway and John Horne who had convinced him that his white intimates were doing him harm. Almost overnight, Mike Tyson was doing the exact opposite of what he had been doing when I first came aboard in May of 1987.

At the same time, the Horne-Holloway force had been firing numerous torpedoes, trying to sink the Tysons' marriage. It didn't take many. During those eight months, Givens and Roper pretty much already had sown the seeds of marital failure by their money-grubbing attitude and the disrespect they displayed toward Mike Tyson. Thus, another Don King goal was close at hand.

Emboldened by the way things were spinning out, Don King decided he safely could fire one of his own missiles and land a direct hit. Before she filed for divorce in Los Angeles, Robin Givens returned to Bernardsville with her mother. At that time, the Tysons still were close to Donald and Ivana Trump. "The Donald" invited the Tysons to spend an entire week aboard the *Trump Princess* so I chauffeured them, along with Holloway and Horne, to Atlantic City where we spent time on both the yacht and at Tyson's Ocean Club penthouse.

One afternoon, Givens went out shopping alone while

we stayed in the penthouse watching television. Holloway and Horne also were there. Tyson was wearing his favorite white t-shirt that said "Iron-Man Mike" which he wouldn't part with no matter how ratty it had gotten over the years. One of my jobs was to make sure that the t-shirt was with us wherever we were travelling or training.

We got buzzed by security from downstairs that Don King had arrived and wanted to come up, and Tyson said it was okay. King said that he had a big promotion going on in Atlantic City that month and wanted Tyson to get involved and go to a press conference. But MT wasn't interested because he was going to spend time hanging out with the Trumps. The two couples had planned to take the *Trump Princess* to the Bahamas for a few days. Don King got wound up when Tyson refused to assist him with his program.

"Goddammit, Mike, you've got to do this! There's millions of dollars involved!"

Don King needed a lot of hype for the upcoming fight, and getting Mike Tyson in front of the cameras would ensure there was plenty. But Tyson held firm, he just wasn't interested because it wasn't one of his fights. King's demeanor and voice changed from irritation to rage.

"I'm tired of your shit with Trump!" King boomed. "Goddammit, Mike, while you're out with Trump on the boat, why don't you ask him why he's *fucking* your wife!"

With that, Don King stormed out of the penthouse apartment. Tyson had the remote in his hand and suddenly threw it violently against the fifty-inch screen, breaking the control. I got scared because I had never seen MT vent his anger like that, except in the ring. The mere thought that his wife was having sex with "The Donald" was unbearable for him. I went to the kitchen to get out of the way. The manner in which Don King had blurted this thing out about Donald Trump and Robin Givens made it sound very believable. Tyson headed for the master bedroom and slammed the door. Fifteen minutes later, Robin sauntered into the penthouse carrying several bags from her shopping trip.

"Mike, I'm home!" she announced.

A few moments later I heard a big smack. As I raced out of the kitchen, I saw Givens on the ground, packages all over the floor. Tyson had let fly an open-handed left to the cheek. MT then stormed out of the apartment just as the maid came in. We tried to help Robin up, but she was dazed, her face still glowing from the smack. When she got to her feet, she started after MT, trying to catch him before he descended in the express elevator. Unable to reach him in time, she came back sobbing and very upset. I tried to explain what had happened, but she didn't want to hear from anybody. When Ruth Roper walked in, Givens screamed to her mother that "I'm not going to take it anymore!" and "this is it!"

John Horne appeared and asked me if I knew where MT had gone.

"If I know him, he's heading for New York."

"Get the limo!" Horne ordered. "You're taking me and Don King to New York."

I got dressed and pulled the Rolls Royce limousine out

of the garage to pick up my passengers. Just then, MT pulled up in the red Lamborghini Countach. I got out to see how he was doing.

"Where you goin' with my limo?" Tyson demanded to know.

When I told him, he ordered me to return it to the garage. "You and me are going to New York in the Countach."

Tyson went inside the Ocean Club to use the bathroom. I got behind the wheel of the Lamborghini and waited for him. Moments later Don King and John Horne appeared at the front door. When they saw me, they started screaming because I didn't have the limo ready for them. Just then, Tyson returned from his trip to the bathroom.

"Don't you yell at him!" MT shouted, jabbing a finger in their direction. "Get your own fucking drivers!"

We left King and Horne in front of the Ocean Club, jumping up and down and yelling like a couple of spoiled brats who didn't get their way, and hit the street in the direction of the Jersey Turnpike. After a few minutes, MT changed his mind and told me to head for the Bernardsville estate instead of the City, put on the headphones to his Walkman, closed his eyes, and listened to rap music the entire trip. After we reached the mansion, MT raced upstairs and went on a terrible rampage, breaking furniture and smashing paintings. He also tore up a lot of Robin's clothes. I begged him to stop, but it was no use so I went downstairs and told the staff to leave our boss to himself. After about an hour I didn't hear anything so I went back up to assess the situation. Like I had seen so many times before, Mike Tyson was asleep, not on the bed, but leaning against its side. I covered him up, and he slept through the night.

The next morning, Robin Givens arrived accompanied by Rory Holloway and John Horne. She went upstairs while Holloway and Horne took me aside.

"You work for Don King, not MT," Holloway told me.

"You shouldn't have left us in the street, motherfucker," Horne added.

I tried to hide my intense dislike for these two ass-holes and said calmly, "I'm confused. I thought Bill Cayton is MT's manager."

Holloway hesitated, then said: "Yeah, whatever."

The next thing that happened was that we heard furniture being tossed out of the master-bedroom window. Robin already had called 911, reporting domestic violence. Soon the local police showed up. They interviewed Tyson who by that time was calm and rational. Because there was no need to arrest him, the patrolmen left as quickly as they had come. Soon after that, Givens descended the staircase with two bags and asked me to take her to Kennedy Airport so she could catch a flight to LA. John Horne jumped in and said he would take her because he had to go to New York anyway. A few days later, Marvin Mitchelson, Robin Givens' attorney, made the announcement that divorce papers had been filed.

A deceptive practice employed by some merchants is to advertise items at very low prices so that customers will race down to their place of business. Once there, the sale items "unfortunately" already have been sold. But since the customers have made the long trip anyway, perhaps the merchant can interest them in something just a little more expensive. That's the classic bait and switch.

Don King baited Givens and Roper into breaking up the Tyson tradition, believing that they could take over Mike Tyson's skyrocketing career and fabulous wealth. Then King, employing the services of Rory Holloway and John Horne, pulled a "switch," which removed Givens and Roper from the game. Don King, chess-player *extraordinaire,* must have been having a good laugh as these pawns marched across the gameboard to his tune. Now, all that was left to do was make the final move, a checkmate which gave Don King total control over heavyweight champion of the world Mike Tyson.

"The Kingdom of Darkness"

Robin Givens left a huge wake of doubt and insecurity behind her when she stormed out of the Bernardsville mansion, and Mike Tyson's life, forever in early October of 1988. The year had started off with great promise for Tyson's personal life. He had the girl of his dreams permanently at his side, and there would be a baby, making them a true family. By June, he knew the joyful sounds of a newborn would not be filling their cavernous home. And his dream girl, while she had taken huge sums of his money, had openly disrespected him and his friends and, worse, had been "doing The Donald," a rich and famous white guy whom Tyson thought he could trust. Now, as the year came to a close, more darkness fell over Mike Tyson's life from which he still has not seen day.

We collect experiences which makes each of us act the way we do. These experiences are like our own personal videotape which starts recording from the moment of birth until, one day, there is no more tape in the camera. Mike Tyson's videotape from his early years contained mostly unhappy experiences, doubts, and insecurities. There had been no father figure and little joy in his childhood home. By age eleven, he had been sent away to do time at the Tryon School, a tough reformatory for the most uncontrollable juvenile delinquents. He wasn't handsome or educated, and he had a high-pitched voice and a lisp. He was facing a life of crime, prison, and even premature death.

But as fate would have it, there would be a radical shift in Mike Tyson's life video. He would be rescued from the reformatory and taken into the home of two elderly white people who raised him as if he were their own son. His father, Cus D'Amato, was a legendary boxing trainer who was convinced, that if Michael Gerard Tyson just would do things right, he would be a world-champion heavyweight fighter. D'Amato had surrounded his son with dedicated people working toward a common goal, the success of Mike Tyson, professional, financial, and personal. And by the beginning of 1988, as the camera kept rolling, the script written by Cus D'Amato, which had saved Mike Tyson's life and made him a very famous and fabulously wealthy young man, still was being followed.

Mike Tyson's life video was turning into a blockbuster movie with a happy ending. But as Don King watched this videotape, he wasn't seeing *It's A Wonderful Life* but rather *Nightmare On 69th Street*, the street where Don King Productions was located. Mike Tyson, managed by Jim Jacobs and Bill Cayton, had been a thorn in DKP for almost two years, knocking out all of It's fighters and capturing the unified heavyweight crown. For Don King, the man who supposedly controlled the world of professional boxing, a world where fabulous sums of money were to be made overnight, not controlling Mike Tyson was excruciatingly unbearable and totally unacceptable.

Don King finally saw the opportunity in 1988 to press the rewind button on the video and erase and record over key portions of the Mike Tyson life experience. By manipulating Givens and Roper, and by employing mercenaries

Holloway and Horne, Don King was able to retitle and rewrite the script. The new screenplay was "Team Tyson," replacing the previous title, "The Tyson Tradition." The original cast, Cus D'Amato, Camille Ewald, Jay Bright, Jim Jacobs, Bill Cayton, Kevin Rooney, Steve Lott, and Matt Baransky, all were to be eliminated. Now there would be only the following main characters listed in order of importance: Don King, Don King Productions, Don King's family, John Horne and Rory Holloway. It wasn't going to be "lights, camera, action" at the filming of "Team Tyson." There were no lights in this Don King "production" as the plot revolved around a foolish and deceitful "rap" designed to keep Mike Tyson in the dark about the most important things in his life.

After John Horne wedged his way into Tyson's life, he utilized Holloway and his long-standing friendship with MT to convince him that "Daddy King" was the saviour. In fact, Don King arranged for a very downcast and lonely Mike Tyson to be baptized in Cleveland, Ohio at the Holy Trinity Baptist Church. The baptism took place on November 27, 1988, presided over by the Reverend Henry Payden, with the assistance of the Reverend Jesse Jackson, while Tyson's new "father figure" proudly looked on. A few days after the ceremony, Mike Tyson fired Kevin Rooney.

Meanwhile, Horne was relentless, rapping constantly to MT that the white man was "evil," and that "you're a nigger, and you've got to hang out with niggers. Let's rock the world because we're a bunch of bad-ass niggers who don't need the white man. We're not going let the white man get away with enslaving us again." This was classic *The World According To Don King.* King knew, valued, and employed the fundamental technique used by the Nazi propaganda machine: *if you repeat something to the masses enough times, they eventually will believe it and act upon it.* In a *New York Daily News* article, former world heavyweight champion Larry Holmes said of Don King: "He treated me like a sucker, but I respect him for getting away with it. You know he's the best. He sells black. Don King is the black KKK, a black supremacist."

John Horne and Rory Holloway filled a huge, gaping hole in Mike Tyson's existence after Robin Givens packed up and left, his dream girl and dream life gone in a flash. He couldn't understand how the marriage could get so messed up so quickly. As a married man, his social life had seemed more fulfilling. After the divorce, MT often would walk around the Bernardsville mansion by himself, dazed, confused, lonely, and vulnerable. In this condition, and without benefit of effective assistance of his counsel, D'Amato, Jacobs, or Rooney, much of this silly "rap" started to make sense to him. It was a perfect time to start rolling the cameras for the first scene in "Team Tyson." And it didn't involve discipline and training. These no longer were priorities, and in fact were excused by the end of 1988. Tyson was convinced by those around him that there was no real threat to his crown. While Don King battled with Bill Cayton for control of the fighter, Horne and Holloway replugged Tyson into "the street" where crime and violence were glorified.

They weren't just doing the regular club scene and staying out all night. Rather, they started getting Tyson to hang out with a "gangsta'-rap" crowd in New York and Los Angeles. Horne and Holloway goaded their famous friend to demonstrate just how "bad" he was wherever they went, resulting in a lot of negative press for Mike Tyson.

I once almost got killed in an East LA club because I made a big mistake. Somebody had reached over and grabbed Tyson by the back of the neck. I shoved that guy away from MT and back into the crowd. Little did I know that my victim was a "Crip," a member of one of the most powerful LA gangs. He made a hand sign, the music suddenly stopped, and I knew I was in deep, deep shit.

"Yo, Mike Tyson," the man said. "Your boy wrong. He gonna' pay now."

"He don't know who you were, man."

It was decided then that I would have to go before the top Crip leader to see how the situation would be resolved. Outside the club, there was a young black kid no more than eighteen, sitting on the back of a brand new Rolls Royce convertible with shiny chrome wheels sitting very low to the ground like a hot rod. As I approached slowly, accompanied by MT and Anthony, I realized the kid was sitting down because he was paralyzed, a gold-plated wheelchair next to the Rolls. Someone later told us he was the "czar" of all the LA gangs. The czar asked what had happened.

"He put his hands on me," said the Crip I had shoved inside the club.

The czar exchanged words with Mike Tyson whom it was very obvious he respected a lot.

"This is my guy," Tyson explained. "He's outta' New York City. He don't know what's goin' on. He was protecting me."

"I'm sorry, sir. I didn't know who he was. I don't understand the colors." I was referring to the Crip gang colors.

Finally, the czar made his ruling. "The guy who touched Mike Tyson. He's gotta' pay." He ordered the guy to step forward so that he could be stomped.

Right in front of us, that poor bastard had the shit beaten out of him by two huge guys. What I did was wrong, but you didn't touch Mike Tyson. This was the court of justice of the street, and the young paralyzed kid was judge and jury.

Part of the plan orchestrated by Don King was to distance Tyson from long-standing friendships which included people from all races, nationalities, and religions. Horne and Holloway constantly were telling him that his old friends "just wanted his money." Soon, King, Horne, and Holloway were convinced they had gotten Mike Tyson just where they wanted him. If Mike Tyson could turn his back on Kevin Rooney, he could turn his back on anybody. Sadly, Tyson began pushing Camille Ewald, his "mother," out of his life. He stopped making frequent visits to his old home in Catskill. The times we did go back to The White House, Tyson would run up to Camille, give her giant bear hugs, sweep her off the ground, and swing her around. "Put me down, Michael!" she would protest because she already was in her eighties and could easily be broken into pieces by Tyson. But Camille loved this powerful show of affection and acted like a little girl whenever she saw MT pulling into the long driveway of The White House.

After greeting Camille, MT would check up on his five dogs, among which were three "royal blood" shar-peis, gifts from the Japanese emperor. Tyson didn't like small dogs, but these were Camille's favorites. And then there were the several hundred pigeons of all types, fliers, tumblers, homing, long-haired. Tyson would walk into the pigeon coop before entering the house. Another ritual was to make sure to bring Camille the famous cheesecake from Junior's bakery on Atlantic Avenue in Brooklyn. I remember how she used to fawn over MT around the clock whenever he spent time back in Catskill. If Tyson were laying on the couch, she would put a pillow under his head. Camille loved cooking meals for a big crowd. She also had a thing about making real hot chocolate, the kind from thick bars. Many times it gave Tyson a bad case of diarrhea, but he never let her know.

When we stayed at The White House, I would notice that there was a daily ritual. Camille and MT would disappear into the den which she had maintained exactly like Cus D'Amato had left it the day he died. They would close the door and speak privately for about an hour, not to be disturbed under any circumstances. They would talk about Cus' advice to Tyson over the years and about what was going on with his life these days. And there was another constant topic, Camille's criticism of MT's constant speeding and growing collection of traffic tickets. She found out that he had gotten two tickets in one night and had to do some community service, going around to Catskill-area schools, lecturing about the dangers of speeding. These same students later would see us outside with the twelve-cylinder five-hundred horsepower Lamborghini, giving us looks of "yeah, right."

"You're going to kill yourselves," she used to warn us. "Why don't you buy normal looking cars?"

Tyson wanted Camille to learn how to drive so she wouldn't be so dependent on others. He told me to teach her how to drive, and she finally did obtain a license. Then Tyson bought her a white Range Rover.

Camille Ewald had a talent for bringing out the "son" in Mike Tyson. Even though he could have bought the local hotel, MT always stayed in his small attic bedroom where he had spent hundreds of hours watching fight films, the screen a sheet tacked to the wall, of some of history's greatest, Dempsey, Marciano, Johnson, Louis. Many of Tyson's techniques, such as the "peek-a-boo" style, were harvested from the wealth contained in these films.

For a brief time after the divorce, before Tyson almost completely turned his back on her, Camille tried to help him heal from the tremendous hurt he was feeling. But his confidence shaken by his failed marriage to a beautiful actress, Tyson started devoting his time exclusively to "gang bangers," street girls from the hood. Horne and Holloway never let Tyson forget that Givens and Trump were out of his league and had treated him as such. I remember the time when MT had the chef hide a tennis bracelet, studded with very large diamonds, in an omelette which Tyson served his wife in the master bedroom. Horne and Holloway got their "friend" into a mentality where romance was for pussies. Tyson was on an emotional rollercoaster, and he began acting very badly toward a lot of people about whom he used to care. He also started showing signs for the first time of losing interest in his career.

Mike Tyson consistently had been fair to me, probably because I had continued to be very professional, respectful and courteous, and always kept my distance. I never acted like I was a part of his inner-circle. Perhaps if I had started calling him "Mike," he would have fired me, but I still was calling him "sir." Meanwhile, Horne and Holloway continued to treat me like shit. They tried everything they could think of to get MT to fire me, but it was one of the very few things they never could accomplish. This made them hate me even more. In fact, Tyson kept adding to my responsibilities and duties after Robin Givens left, depending on me more and more to keep his life organized. He trusted me and knew I got results. I now was taking all his phonecalls, managing the staff, and scheduling his private appointments and public appearances. He also relied on my judgment in selecting his wardrobe.

The next match was on February 25, 1989, against Great Britain's Frank Bruno at the Las Vegas Hilton. It was my first trip to the neon city. Tyson's corner had new people. By now, Rooney, Lott, and Baransky were gone, and Aaron Snowell was the new first trainer. It was obvious that it was not the same Mike Tyson who entered the ring that night. In the first round, Bruno connected with two hooks which made MT stagger. Although by the fifth round he had disposed of Bruno, it was obvious that his lack of training was taking its toll. His performance was sloppy, failing to effectively employ his trademark techniques which had made him heavyweight champion, patience, cunning, rapid side-to-side moves, and rapid combination strikes.

When we returned to the East, Mike Tyson didn't want to continue living at the Bernardsville estate. He wanted to remove every item from the mansion because they reminded him of his failed marriage. He wanted to strip the mansion bare, leaving it an empty shell, much like his life was at that time. Robin Givens was notified and made arrangements to pick up a number of things. I sent the balance to storage.

As his chauffeur, waiting hours for him as he used to stroll aimlessly around the empty mansion, I probably was the only person to know how much Tyson continued to suffer deep inside. He always had been in love with Robin Givens and blamed himself for many of the problems leading to the breakup of his marriage. Mike Tyson was the heavyweight champion of the world, undefeated in thirty-six professional bouts, but he had lost the battle to keep his first marriage together.

The Ocean Club in Atlantic City again became our home base. Tyson wasn't training during this time, the next fight, against Carl Williams, not scheduled until mid-summer. With Kevin Rooney out of the picture, no time was being spent polishing Tyson's techniques. My boss still would run in the morning, but there was nobody coaching him. Mike Tyson had become his own trainer.

What *was* getting a thorough workout during this period was Tyson's social life. With Horne and Holloway around all the time serving as cheerleaders, Tyson started partying around the clock. To avoid the risk of another deep wound, like the one he had suffered with Robin Givens, Tyson now was seeking only brief encounters with women, not romantic relationships. The club scene provided a revolving door for sex, picking up women and doing the *wild thing*, gang-banging in the back of the limo, then dropping the girls off back at the clubs. I soon realized that John Horne never took advantage of the plentiful pussy passing through the rear of the limo. However, Tyson pal Eddie Murphy frequently would join up with Tyson to hit the club scene and participate in the gang-banging. I once risked asking Murphy for his autograph which I was going to give to my mother who adored him. I should have known better because he never yet had acknowledged my existence. "Hey, don't bother me with that shit, man," he said, pushing the paper out of my hand. After that night, I never again have asked a celebrity for an autograph, nor have I ever wanted to be photographed with one.

As we headed into the summer of 1989, it was unclear who officially controlled the career of Mike Tyson, Don King or Bill Cayton. The Carl "Truth" Williams fight was coming up on July 21 at the Atlantic City Convention Center. This was going to be his second and only other fight of 1989. There literally were both Cayton and King people in Tyson's corner that night when Tyson knocked out the "Truth" in the first round.

Tyson really wasn't interested in getting involved. He really didn't care to know anything about Don King or Bill Cayton, or anyone for that matter, at this point. To him everything already had turned into bullshit a long time ago. As far as he was concerned, he wasn't going to do anything until taking on the number one contender, Evander Holyfield. His thinking was: "Fuck it. I'll just hang out for awhile."

After the Williams fight, Mike Tyson wanted a change. He spent a lot of peaceful time with friends from his old neighborhood. On Christmas Eve of that year, I took him to the house of that close childhood friend from Brownsville known as "Ouie." When we first arrived at Ouie's house, as usual I remained outside with the limo. Apparently, MT still was so preoccupied with everything that was going on around him, and so relieved that again he was going to spend time with an old friend, that he forgot I was outside waiting for further instructions. I remained there for three days.

Sitting by the fireplace with Ouie, MT travelled back to the old days and, in so doing, found a brief refuge from the darkness of "The Kingdom." They didn't talk about money or contracts or upcoming fights, and they didn't do the club scene. A lot of family and friends stopped by, it seemed sometimes by the busloads, during this time at Ouie's. Tyson enjoyed visiting with everybody and playing with the kids. He felt comfortable in this atmosphere, really chilling for the first time since I could remember.

For awhile we didn't hear anything from Don King or John Horne. They were busy in Japan trying to promote a fight between Tyson and James "Buster" Douglas. On the third day of waiting for MT to emerge from Ouie's house, I got paged by John Horne. He and Don King were back in the City and wanted to speak with Mike Tyson. I went up to the front door and knocked. Ouie answered and I told him about the page. A couple of minutes later, Tyson appeared at the door.

"Shit, Rudy! You've been sittin' here for three days in the fucking car?"

"Sir, Don King and John Horne are looking for you."

"I don't want to talk to them. Say you don't know where I'm at."

I called Horne back and asked for a number where they'd be at so that, in case I reached MT, he could call them. Horne gave me the number for the cellular phone in Don King's limousine. After awhile, Horne called Tyson's own cellular phone. MT handed it to me. He was worried that they were going to track him down at Ouie's place. Therefore, I related to Horne that we were on the road near a certain exit of the Long Island Expressway, sending him on a wild goose chase away from Ouie's house. However, Tyson still was worried that they eventually would show up.

"Shit, man, I've gotta' get outta' here," he said, pulling on some clothes.

As we sped along the Expressway back toward the City, Don King's limousine passed us, then dropped back. A few seconds later, the car phone rang.

"Goddammit, Rudy!" John Horne screamed. "You better stop that limo!"

"Don't stop, Rudy!" Tyson shouted. "Keep going!"

I accelerated but King's limousine, headlights annoyingly flashing at us, was bearing down hard.

"What do I do, sir?"

"Lose them!"

I jumped the limo onto an embankment and hung a u-turn, almost flipping the limo over. Now we were headed east back toward Long Island. I looked over and saw King's limo still heading west. Don King had his head stuck out of the window, his hair spiked straight up like a porcupine, shaking a fist angrily at me. The car phone and my beeper went off simultaneously, MT laughing uncontrollably in the back. I wondered what would have happened if I had wrecked this expensive automobile. After a dozen rings, Tyson finally answered the phone.

"What, Don, what? Fuck, no, I'm not going to Japan. I'm fighting Holyfield!"

Mike Tyson was supposed to fight the premier challenger, Evander Holyfield, in Vancouver, British Columbia in two months. But the Buster Douglas fight Don King was promoting in Japan would make DKP a lot of money. For Mike Tyson, earning a few million more wasn't a priority. He already had wealth. Tyson wanted to fight and defeat the number one contender as soon as possible because that's what a champion was *supposed* to do. He hung up on Don King.

"Don't answer the fucking phone no more. Take me to the apartment in the City."

As I waited in front of the Marlborough House at 245 East 40th Street in Manhattan, I wondered how the rest of the night was going to shake out. It wasn't long before Don King's limo pulled up, and King and John Horne jumped out.

"You're fired!" King shouted at me. "And your games are over, motherfucker!" He turned to Horne. "Take the keys from the limo and throw that motherfucker out!"

I locked the doors before Horne could reach me. He started banging on the windows, screaming "Open the fucking door, give me the fucking keys!" I sat there listening to the radio and ignored him. Horne finally gave up and went inside the building. About two hours later, MT, King, and Horne came outside. Tyson got into the limo.

"We're going to fucking Japan," he told me. "So we've gotta' get ready."

Tyson had been transformed in this short time, becoming submissive to the wishes of King and Horne. It was as if they held some special power or control over him which could take away his will to resist what-

128

ever they wanted him to do.

I drove back to Bernardsville where MT wanted to pick up a few items that remained there, including luggage and a steamer trunk which had belonged to Robin Givens. Then Tyson told me to head for the Catskills for one of the few visits he made to The White House after things started going badly. We stayed there for three days, then made the trip back to Manhattan. We arrived at DKP on East 69th Street and the darkness of The Kingdom.

Having come down with a severe case of the flu running around the Catskills, I stayed in the City while Team Tyson took off for Japan to participate in promotions and to train for the February 11, 1990, Buster Douglas fight at the Tokyo Dome. After I had chauffeured everybody to the airport, I went to see my mother. It was the first time I really had spent any time with her since May of 1987 when I went to work full-time for Mike Tyson. Sometimes I would be only a few blocks away from her building in Spanish Harlem, but working for Mike Tyson was a twenty-four-hour job. I never wanted to violate Tyson's trust by doing personal things. I would call her a lot and always say: "Mom, I'll see you soon." By now my father had been released from Sing Sing and was back living with my Mom. So I was able to spend a couple of weeks with them both. I had been to see my Dad a few times, usually taking one of my girlfriends along who thought it was "cool" to visit a big prison like Sing Sing and to have a father who was a convicted drug dealer doing hard time.

When Tyson called from Tokyo, he told me that I could use his apartment at the Marlborough House. I recovered from my flu very quickly, put the limo in the garage, and pulled out the black Ferrari. Tyson also owned a rare Lamborghini "jeep," originally built for the King of Saudi Arabia. It had a 200-gallon fuel tank, was bullet-proof, and had room for four passengers and six bodyguards. It was designed to do 200 m.p.h. over the desert. Made of 3/4" steel, it was so heavy it couldn't be towed. Sometimes I would drive that "jeep" around the City if there was a lot of snow on the ground. It was such an unusual and exotic vehicle that the "jeep" once had been loaned to the crew filming an episode of *Miami Vice*. These two weeks before I joined Tyson in Japan were going to be my first vacation in three years. By now I was a "celebrity" in my old neighborhood, and I enjoyed being a "big shot" for a few days, cruising around town in the Ferrari with my old buddies.

Don King was milking the Japan trip for every penny he could get, having organized each day of Mike Tyson's schedule for the purpose of raking in the bucks. It didn't matter that the hectic pace wasn't in Tyson's best career interests. Somebody said King was going to haul in $100 million during this Japanese promotional tour. King had Tyson running all over the country, and by the time I got there, my boss was exhausted. Everywhere MT and his crew went there were multitudes of people taking pictures. Tyson was used to locking himself inside the gym in preparation for a fight. This wasn't possible anymore now that Don King had taken over. Rather,

Tyson's workouts in Japan had become public spectacles. With all the curious onlookers everywhere we went and trained, I felt like we were in some kind of "freak show." We had been to Japan before, the Tony Tubbs match on March 21, 1988, but MT had trained in the States and only spent a short time away from our home base before the fight. Now, Tyson was spending more than a month before the Douglas fight doing promotions to make DKP a ton of money. As consolation, whenever there was free time at the hotel, MT was banging geisha girls.

Adding to the problems was the matter of diet. Tyson was having some very real problems with the local food. He was having frequent bouts of diarrhea, and his weight was fluctuating a lot. Our hosts were very gracious and eager to please, but it was made known to Tyson that refusing to eat dishes offered to him during the promotions would be considered an insult to the Japanese. Once we were eating a particular dish and later found out it was rattlesnake. Tyson also ate some blowfish which made him very sick. When he once requested a bowl of fried rice, he was served beautifully-sculpted but very tiny cubes.

"We're gonna' die of hunger," I used to say after too many "displays" like this. On this issue, I didn't feel like keeping my mouth shut. We started checking out the local American fast food, like McDonald's, but it didn't taste like anything we were used to back in the States.

Unable to take it any longer, and with the fight still weeks away, one day MT said: "Man, get me Chef Early. I

131

need some crunchy fried chicken, potato s, and grits."

The next day, the tall, distinguished black chef arrived with a large supply of chicken, ribs, and steaks. Tyson was delighted to see his "James Brown-of-soul-food" cook. Chef Early had been hired by Tyson when his predecessor didn't cooperate about having enough Captain Crunch on hand. With that in mind, his first day on board Chef Early brought with him a hugh supply of the cereal. Tyson always used to say: "Where's my CK man, gotta' have my CK." We used to fight over the prizes in the cereal boxes. Sometimes me and Anthony would steal them before our boss got to the table, and he would hunt us down to get them back.

Chef Early wanted to use the facilities in our Tokyo hotel. Apparently, this was an insult to the hotel's chefs, causing a big stir. After negotiations were conducted, and apologies duly tendered, the Japanese conditionally surrendered. The kitchen was handed over to Chef Early as long he agreed to teach them the art of soul-food cooking. This was so they would be ready to better serve the famous fighter the next time he came to Japan. We ate like kings once Chef Early got things going in the kitchen.

It was in Japan that Mike Tyson learned about the benefits of aged ginseng root. We went to a farm where high-quality product was available, and MT spent $5,000 for some very old ginseng root. Apparently, it made you burn calories faster, and it sure made MT sweat a lot. Ginseng root also supposedly detoxified the system in the process. After he drank a tea made from dissolving the root in boiling water,

Tyson pissed black with a very funky smelly-feet odor. But he also felt very good afterwards. When we got back from Japan, Tyson continued to purchase aged ginseng root and drank three cups of the tea each day.

It was getting close to the match date, and Tyson still hadn't gotten into a real fight-training mode. All the training so far had been to play to the cameras. Don King kept assuring the undefeated champion that there was nothing to worry about. Douglas was a bum who couldn't possibly beat the world champ. The odds-makers had made it a whopping 42-1 long shot. Tyson kept insisting that he should be fighting the only real contender, Evander Holyfield. He wanted to dispose of Holyfield as soon as possible. And Don King kept trying to convince him that Holyfield wasn't a *contender*. Holyfield *wasn't* a contender because he was controlled by Dan Duva and *not* Don King. As DKP kept revving up the jampacked promotional pace in Japan, Tyson started shifting his interest away from the Douglas fight and in the direction of getting more blowjobs.

Whether on a level playing field on February 11, 1990, Buster Douglas was a real contender against Tyson will never be known because two days before the fight the field tilted. Buster Douglas' mother, Lula, had died a few days before. And the mother of his young son had just learned she had a life-threatening kidney disease. While Tyson was cavorting around Japan for weeks with Don King, his image spread every day all over the tv and press, Buster Douglas, had been training back in the States. Now, as he readied for the fight,

Douglas, sitting in a Tokyo hotel, was a very lonely man with a one-way-ticket to nowhere. Nobody even had cared to photograph the challenger at his weigh-in the day before the fight. Oscar de la Hoya had surprised the boxing world when he won a gold medal. He had promised his own mother he would put a gold medal around her tombstone. A hungry man has an advantage over a man with a full stomach.

Unexpected things began happening right from the first bell. Douglas started landing rights on Tyson like nobody ever had witnessed before. At the end of the second round, Douglas hit Tyson with a hard uppercut to the chin. Tyson recovered ground in the third with a big left body punch. Douglas wasn't shaken because he soon wobbled the champ with a chopping right, causing Tyson's left eye to begin swelling. In the eighth, Tyson landed one of his classic uppercuts which knocked Douglas to the canvas with six seconds left in the round. The referee, Octavio Meyran Sanchez, started counting two beats behind the knockdown timekeeper. Keeping his attention on Meyran's hands, as he was supposed to do, Douglas waited until the nine-count before he rose. The bell then ended the round. This was going to cause one of the biggest controversies in boxing history at the end of the match.

In the next round, Douglas pushed Tyson into the ropes and landed four big punches. Tyson was shaken, his head flopping backward, his left eye completely closing. At 1:23 into the tenth, Douglas hit Tyson with a right uppercut, two more punches, then a chopping left hook which dispatched the champion to the floor. Never having been knocked down in his professional career, Tyson stretched out his right glove and swept it along the canvas. Finding his mouthpiece, he was so dazed that he put it in backwards, and struggled to his feet, falling into Meyran's arms. The fight was over.

This was a huge disaster for Don King. Suddenly, he no longer controlled the heavyweight champion of the world. This meant that the eventual pay-per-view match with Evander Holyfield, worth an estimated $70 million, wasn't going to happen according to plan. Now the championship fight would be between Holyfield and Douglas, two non-champs. By being greedy, first wanting to reap millions by promoting Tyson in Japan for weeks without training him properly and then putting him up against a non-contender, Don King inadvertently had dethroned his heavyweight meal-ticket and bushwhacked his own biggest payday yet. King had to mount an immediate campaign to have the match nullified as a result of the late eighth-round Meyran count against a floored Douglas. However, the tactic didn't work. James "Buster" Douglas officially was declared the new heavyweight champion of the world.

After the fight, Douglas told a tv interviewer that he had won the fight "because of my mother, God bless her heart." The papers called the fight "the biggest upset in boxing history. *Time* magazine declared "a story like this happens only in the movies. To be exact, it happens only in *Rocky* movies." Tyson's post-fight statement to the press simply was: "Greater fighters than I have lost."

Mike Tyson's left eye was swollen the size of a baseball from the blows inflicted upon him by Buster Douglas. Tyson was very concerned because several doctors mentioned he might have suffered permanent eye damage. It took a couple of weeks before it finally opened up enough so he could see. During that time, I had to hold his hand wherever he walked. When we arrived back at Kennedy Airport, a swarm of media and sports writers was waiting for us. Tyson had lost the heavyweight crown, and he desperately wanted to avoid everybody and head straight for the Catskills. Ten days later, MT learned that his sister, Denise, whom he loved very much, had suffered a heart attack and died. She was only twenty-six-years old. Still physically hurting very much from the Douglas fight, we attended her funeral in Brooklyn. It was only the second time I had seen Mike Tyson with tears during the three years I had known him. After the funeral, we returned to The White House where Tyson spent another four weeks quietly recuperating. As usual, Camille gave him every ounce of her love and attention to help him through these tragedies, and many old friends stopped by to give him their love and support. Fortunately, MT's eye completely healed.

Mike Tyson was very angry and disgusted with Don King after the *fiasco* in Japan. He should never have been put in that situation, a hectic promotional tour schedule lasting many weeks without any effective training for a championship fight. Don King had driven MT around for weeks like a fancy sports car, then parked him, leaving the lights on all night, the battery completely drained by the next morning. Meanwhile, Don King was starting to feel the full effect of his blunder. The Mirage, a gorgeous Las Vegas hotel, decided to sponsor the next heavyweight championship fight between Buster Douglas and Evander Holyfield. It would be the first time that the site for a heavyweight fight *also* would be its promoter. Being cheap and expecting a lackluster performance, Don King only had signed Douglas to a one-fight deal to save himself a few bucks. This now was a big problem for King because Douglas, instead of Tyson, was the new "*baddest* guy on the planet." Just like Douglas had done to Tyson in the tenth round at the Tokyo Dome, Don King had been knocked out of the Douglas-Holyfield fight before he knew what had hit him.

Incredibly, things turned from bad to worse for Don King. Holyfield later would knock out Douglas in the first round of that fight at The Mirage, now making the Duva-controlled fighter "the *baddest* guy on the planet." Don King was a man unwilling to put on a professional fight unless he controlled *both sides* of the ring. He wanted it to be like the days when, if you didn't use Kodak, you didn't take pictures. Don King wanted it *all*. And to have it all, of course you needed to control the champ. Years before, as Joe Frazier lay on the canvas, Don King bolted into the ring, stepped over his own fighter's unconscious body, on his way to make a deal with the new champ, George Foreman. After the Buster Douglas victory over Mike Tyson, George Foreman, now forty-one and on the rebound into professional boxing at mid-life, chirped: "*Humpty Dumpty sat on the wall / Humpty Dumpty had a great fall / All of Don King's horses and all of Don King's men / Couldn't put Humpty together again.*"

Don King knew it wasn't likely he'd be able to lure Holyfield away from the Duvas. King already had snatched many of their fighters, and they weren't about to let it happen again. But there was nobody else left in the DKP stable for Tyson to fight. Unless, of course, Tyson was hyped as "a former heavyweight champion" who needed to fight other non-champs working his way back to the top. In the interim, there always was the chance that Evander Holyfield would lose the crown, thus permitting DKP to put on a championship match where it controlled both fighters.

One day while we were spending time at The White House, we watched Evander Holyfield win a fight. Afterward, Holyfield was interviewed and asked "so, what's next?"

"I'm gonna' fight Tyson," he said. "He's a girl, and I'm *Real Deal* Holyfield. And Tyson's not the *baddest* guy on the planet."

Tyson's angry expression at that moment reminded me of Sylvester Stallone in the *Rocky* movie when, during pre-fight hype, "Mr. T" made insulting comments about Rocky's wife. "I'm gonna' fuck Holyfield up!" Tyson shouted skyward.

You don't call MT a "girl" in front of anybody, let alone millions of tv viewers. From that day forward, there was only one thing on MT's mind: *kick Holyfield's ass right away*. And nothing was going to stop Mike Tyson from having his day with Evander "Real Deal" Holyfield. Or so I believed at the time.

Don King went to work on Mike Tyson right away so that there would be no championship fight between him and heavyweight champion Evander Holyfield whom DKP didn't control. After promising Tyson constantly that he soon would get his chance with Holyfield, Don King convinced MT that he first needed two "comeback" fights. It was really all about King buying time, desperately praying that Evander Holyfield would lose the title while Tyson attended to other business. MT reluctantly agreed but kept wondering, if he was still ranked number one, why shouldn't he be going straight to the ring to prove it with Holyfield?

Mike Tyson's first fight on "The Road Back" was against Henry Tillman. It took place at Caesar's Palace in Las Vegas on June 16, 1990 and was broadcast on HBO. Don King had said about Tyson before the fight: "We just want to let you know he's alive and kicking." After the Buster Douglas upset, the media had been publishing numerous stories about Tyson's heavy drinking, late nights, fast cars, pretty women, divorce, manic-depression, and an alleged suicide attempt.

Tyson was interviewed before the fight and was asked what went wrong in Japan. "I made a big mistake. I didn't respect the championship at that particular time. I was in good shape physically, but emotionally I wasn't right. Basically, I screwed up. I'm no less of a fighter. I'm not on the verge of killing myself."

As the first bell sounded, Tyson bolted out of his corner and went on the attack. Tillman landed a few punches to

Tyson's body, but they looked and sounded like he was hitting a brick wall. At 2:47 into the first round, Tyson landed a lightning overhand right to Tillman's temple, knocking him out. MT showed the critics that night that he still could be a ferocious fighter. There was no question but that Tyson was hungry after his embarrassing loss to Buster Douglas in Tokyo four months before. "I fought the way I always fight," he told the press. "I just fought with a little more appetite."

When Tillman went down, the first one to rush to his side was Mike Tyson. "Me and Henry are very good friends," Tyson told reporters. "I just wanted to make sure he was OK. We're friends. It just so happens that we are good friends in the same business."

The next and only other fight for Mike Tyson for the balance of 1990 was another "Road to Recovery" match, against Alex "The Destroyer" Stewart on December 8 at Atlantic City's Convention Center, also carried on HBO. Don King had arranged an undercard junior-welterweight title bout, Mexico's Julio Cesar Chavez against Ahn Kyung-Duk of South Korea. Chavez was 72-0 with 59 knockouts.

Before the fight his new trainer, Richard Giachetti, responded to comments that Tyson's trademark "peek-a-boo, bobbing, and weaving" were noticeably absent from the Tillman bout.

"We haven't done anything to change Mike's style," Giachetti said. "It's just the natural evolution in a fighter."

By the time the Stewart fight rolled around, Tyson had gotten himself into better shape, now weighing in at 217 whereas he had ballooned up to almost 230 a few months before. Some said he looked as good as when he made short work of Michael Spinks, knocking him out in the first 91 seconds, back on June 27, 1988, at the same Convention Center.

Within eight seconds of the first bell, Tyson connected with a right to Stewart's head, bringing him to the floor. Stewart went down once again with another right before the final, match-winning blow at 2:27 into the first round. Tyson had been so wound up to finish off Stewart that, 50 seconds into the fight, he fell on his stomach when he missed with one of his lightning jabs. By the time the fight ended, Tyson had knocked Stewart down three times and had connected with 21 out of his 46 swings. Stewart swung out 18 times but landed only four punches on Tyson. When Tyson felled Stewart with the final blow, Don King rushed into the ring screaming "We're back, we're back, watch our smoke now!" Tyson earned $2.5 million and Stewart $375,000. Julio Cesar Chavez also won his fight by a knockout, at 2:14 into the third round.

"I just wanted to explode on him," Tyson later told reporters. "I was hungry."

The fabulous Mirage Hotel in Las Vegas, under the dynamic leadership of Steve Wynn, had agreed to sponsor James "Buster" Douglas in a heavyweight title bout with Evander Holyfield after Douglas upset Tyson in Tokyo. Suddenly, Don King realized there was a new kid on the block, a block which he desperately had tried to control by erecting toll booths at both ends. Now it looked like the new kid had slipped by without first paying the toll. Don King needed to have a heart-to-heart as soon as possible. Immediately after the Tyson-Stewart fight, King approached Steve Wynn with the idea of holding Tyson fights at the hotel on an exclusive basis. Tyson would fight nowhere except The Mirage.

It was an opportune moment to make the overture. A few weeks before, Mirage-sponsored Buster Douglas had performed miserably against Evander Holyfield who now had become the heavyweight champion. Holyfield was controlled by the Duvas who already had a relationship with another Vegas hotel. Don King's pitch to Steve Wynn: "What you need is a promoter like me at a time like this. I know this business better than anybody. Pay-per-view is the megabucks wave of the future. Forget HBO. I have something cooking with Showtime. All you have to do is leave things in my hands." DKP had been negotiating a deal with Showtime executives who enthusiastically embraced King's vision. The idea was to offer Tyson fights live for around $40 on a pay-per-view basis, and to broadcast reruns a week later to regular Showtime subscribers.

King got a reluctant Tyson to send a message to his fans, that he was walking away from HBO, Atlantic City, and Donald Trump for good, destination KingVision/Showtime, Las Vegas, and Don King Productions even though Bill Cayton still was his manager of record until early 1992 when his current contract expired. Three days after the Alex Stewart fight we were on a plane to Las Vegas.

I'll never forget that first day as we approached The Mirage Hotel. Its beauty is a magnet, pulling you inside where its luxurious interior consumes you. At the entrance, there are lagoons and a live volcano which every few minutes erupts spewing smoke and fire one hundred feet into the sky. Its "White Tiger Habitat" contains rare and exotic white tigers for the Internationally famous "Siegfried and Roy Show." In the front lobby there is a 20,000 gallon aquarium stocked with sharks, rays, and angelfish. It made me feel very small as I strolled through the hotel on the way to Steve Wynn's executive offices. In sharp contrast to the rest of the hotel, Mr. Wynn's office was very modest and functional. There already was a meeting in progress, but Mr. Wynn ushered us in and enthusiastically shook our hands. Steve Wynn was a very great fan of Mike Tyson and had been following the progress of his career for some time. He expressed to Tyson that he loved to watch him box. Mr. Wynn called in his secretary and instructed her to make arrangements for us to stay in a VIP suite on the top floor next to Michael Jackson who had a permanent residence there.

Mr. Wynn's personal assistant set things in motion for us, giving us a grand tour of the facilities, obtaining security cards, and providing keys to the snack bar which was more like a well-stocked kitchen. She also introduced us to the twenty-four-hour maid and butler service assigned to the VIP suites. We were informed that we could not carry weapons in the hotel but would be able to check them at the VIP reception desk and retrieve them whenever necessary.

Finally, the personal assistant asked us if we had any special needs. I told her that Mr. Tyson had several cars, including a limousine, and we liked to park these vehicles in front of buildings we stayed in for easy access. The personal assistant mentioned that no one, not even Mr. Wynn, was allowed to park in front of The Mirage. However, because Mr. Wynn considered Mike Tyson a very special guest, he had decided to make an exception. An area would be cordoned off in front of the hotel where Team Tyson could station all of its vehicles. So it wasn't long before we were displaying a brand new ten-pack Lincoln stretch limo, the black Lamborghini Diablo, a Ferrari Koenig worth $750,000, a twelve-cylinder six-speed BMW 850si, and two corvettes, one canary yellow, the other cherry red. It looked like an exotic car dealership. A security guard was assigned just to watch over this inventory. We were thankful for his attentions and got him ring-side seats for the family.

Like always, I was committed to be courteous and thoughtful wherever we went and with whomever we dealt. Because most people had to go through me before they could deal with Tyson, I wanted to make sure that I made a good impression. If I acted like an asshole, then people surely would believe Mike Tyson was a much bigger one. When people served us well, our philosophy was to return their attentions with thanks and generosity. We always conducted ourselves in this fashion at The Mirage, and soon all the employees knew we were "good guys." With MT living at The Mirage, a great deal of interest was generated in the

145

hotel, and thousands of visitors hoped to catch a glimpse of the world-famous heavyweight boxer. We wore our Jeff Hamilton-crafted leather Tyson jackets everywhere we went in Vegas. Leather wasn't worn much there, and we soon were easily recognized from a distance, people shouting "there go the Tyson guys!"

Things seemed like they were pretty much on track during January and February, 1991, our first two months in Vegas. Tyson was in better spirits after his decisive victories against Henry Tillman and Alex Stewart. Even though there still were ongoing legal battles about who really controlled Mike Tyson, as usual my boss stayed out of the fray. Instead, as long as bills were being paid and he had spending money, MT was content. Introduced to designer clothes by ex-girl-friend and supermodel Naomi Campbell, Tyson continued to spend large sums of money on his wardrobe. He now bought almost exclusively at Gianni Versace. There were $2,700 shirts, $2,000 belts, $7,000 leather pants, and once a leather bomber jacket for $78,000. Because I was in charge of purchasing his clothing, the sales clerks salivated whenever I arrived, making me feel like the Richard Gere character in *Pretty Woman*. MT would have me buy three of everything so that he would have a complete wardrobe at each of his three residences, the Marlborough House in New York City, the penthouse on Wilshire Boulevard in Beverly Hills, and the sprawling estate in Southington, Ohio.

As we approached the March 18 fight against Donovan "Razor" Ruddock, Tyson was determined to remain focused on his training with Richard Giachetti, anticipating that he would get his shot at the title with Evander Holyfield very soon. Things were going better for me as well. I started dating several gorgeous young ladies who worked at the Mirage.

On March 18, 1991, in the Mirage hotel's outdoor arena, the Tyson-Ruddock fight ended in a fashion which nobody had expected, except perhaps Don King. In the first round, Tyson charged out at the well-muscled 228-pound Ruddock who towered over Tyson at 6'3", but Ruddock survived Tyson's attack. In the second, Ruddock did go down for an eight-count, but only by inadvertently hooking Tyson's leg causing him to fall. Finally, in the next round, Tyson connected with a hook after Ruddock missed a right hand. Dazed and confused, Ruddock hit the canvas and stayed down while referee Richard Steele counted out six. The bell rang as Ruddock sought the refuge of his corner, raising his arms to tell the crowd "I'm alright." In the fifth and sixth rounds, Ruddock landed a number of punches on Tyson, but they didn't seem to faze Tyson. However, late into the sixth, Ruddock did connect with two left hooks and a right. Tyson got in close and grabbed Ruddock who, breaking free, found paydirt with another right. Tyson was very upset and pointed to his chin, meaning "come on if you want some more." It wasn't smart to do that because Ruddock got in another right causing Tyson's head to snap back just as the bell sounded. Later Tyson would say it felt like a "mule kick."

When the seventh round started, Tyson showed that he was very pissed off at his performance and beckoned Ruddock forward. Soon MT had landed two blows to the hips which, by their boos, some fans believed were illegally low. With only a minute left in the round, Tyson attempted to make up for lost time and drilled Ruddock into the ropes.

He combined with a body punch and hook to Ruddock's head which snapped back violently. Ruddock staggered back to his corner with raised gloves. Tyson scored two more direct hits, a right and a left, again driving Ruddock into the ropes. Referee Steele suddenly rushed in and grabbed Tyson with both arms. Steele seemed more preoccupied with preventing MT from causing further damage than whether Ruddock was in danger. Suddenly and unexpectedly, Steele waved that the fight was over.

Ruddock was shocked. "What!" he yelled at the referee which served as a battle cry for his cornermen. Led by brother-manager Delroy Ruddock, they charged into the ring, including Ruddock promoter Murad Muhammad. Tyson dealt with this show simply by shouting "That's bullshit, that's bullshit." Giachetti, hoping to prevent any harm to the referee, lunged at Delroy Ruddock and told him to "cool it." Murad Muhammad, now covering Delroy, sucker-punched Giachetti who went down, and then kicked him four times. Bright-green jackets from the hotel's security forces suddenly filled the ring, and referee Richard Steele was quickly shepherded to safety. A few brawls were going on in the ring, but the two fighters had retreated to the corners.

Steele later declared that Ruddock had been unable to defend himself, giving him no choice but to stop the fight. "People just get out of hand because of the simple fact they don't understand boxing. They must come to see someone get hurt seriously or death."

Murad Muhammad violently disagreed. "All we want

is justice," he said after the spectacle in the ring had stopped. Prior to the match, Muhammad had been uneasy about Steele serving as referee due to his close ties to Don King. His concern was, that if his fighter started scoring against Tyson, then Steele would find an opportunistic moment to eliminate Ruddock, leaving Tyson an undeserving winner. Muhammad threatened legal action but later agreed that a rematch would be an acceptable alternative.

Tyson wasn't a happy camper, to say the least, with the way things turned out. He was convinced that a few more seconds in the ring with Ruddock would have left no doubt about the winner. But the Tyson-Ruddock "rematch" solution to the controversy was exactly what Don King wanted. If Tyson had scored a definitive victory against Ruddock, then King would have had to put up or shut up about getting Tyson his day with Holyfield. King couldn't let this happen because he didn't control both ends of the street. The Duvas owned the rights to a Holyfield-Tyson fight and, therefore, would decide where the match would be held. This meant that the championship fight would not take place at The Mirage.

By early June, Dan Duva, Evander Holyfield's promoter, offered the record amount of $51.1 million for a Tyson-Holyfield fight to be scheduled for October or November at Ceasar's Palace. It wasn't going to happen. Bill Cayton, who on paper still was Tyson's manager until February 12, 1992, saw exactly what was happening.

"King uses Tyson's drawing power to make these other fights and pays exorbitant prices to his stable of fighters like

Chavez and Simon Brown," Cayton was quoted in the June 24, 1991 issue of *Sports Illustrated*.

Cayton particularly had in mind the $2.5 million paid for the Tyson-Ruddock undercard, put on by Don King, with junior-welterweight Julio Cesar Chavez, at the expense of the Tyson's own purse. There also was another DKP fighter on the undercard, Simon Brown, who received $1.5 million. KingVision/Showtime had revenues of about $28 million. The whole affair grossed around $41 million. Don King's share was around $9 million after all expenses, including payment to each of his fighters. Tyson's take supposedly was $5.7 million. Had Mike Tyson continued to follow the strategy originally mapped out by Bill Cayton, he would have been guaranteed $8.5 million in a multifight deal which had been set up with HBO. But all that had been torpedoed by Don King when he enticed Mike Tyson away from HBO and over to KingVision/Showtime.

When asked about Tyson-Ruddock II, Cayton said: "This Ruddock rematch just compounds the stupidity. Tyson should have fought for his title by now."

As time marched on during 1991, Mike Tyson began questioning more and more why he was wasting time with other matches before getting to have his day with Evander "Real Deal" Holyfield. It made no difference to Tyson that there would be less money, or any money for that matter, if the match were held at another Vegas hotel or in an alley. MT wanted to fight Holyfield now because that's what a champion was *supposed* to do. The press got wind of Tyson's increasingly aggressive attitude toward Don King, including rumors that there had been physical confrontations between the two. King refused a request by *Sports Illustrated* to either confirm or deny. However, he did tell *USA Today* that he and Tyson argued.

"When we do," said King. "I cuss him out and he cusses me out, and it ain't no boxing match. Ain't nobody screw with me, man. Part of my job as promoter and friend ain't to get my fanny whipped. I don't submit to that. I'm not afraid of Mike, and he's not afraid of me. We don't have to come to blows to resolve personal differences."

It wasn't long before a date would be set for the Tyson-Ruddock II fight, again to take place at the outdoor arena of the The Mirage Hotel. If I had been told that I wouldn't be around to see it, I wouldn't have believed it. But then again, I had been wrong before.

"From the Darkness Comes a Whisper"

We remained in Las Vegas for a few weeks after the first Tyson-Ruddock fight, hoping to get in some rest and relaxation. Don King also spent time there and started an annoying habit of storming into our quarters, yelling "Goddammit, Mike, you're gonna' watch something else besides those fucking cartoons!" It was then we learned that King had an extensive collection of documentary films dealing with World War II and the Nazi movement. He would pull out Tyson's "Tom and Jerry" and "Roadrunner" cassettes and instead stick in videos of Hitler and the Nazis. King sent me off to Vegas' main library to look for more films and even once had me fly all the way back to New York just to retrieve part of his video collection from his mid-town Manhattan townhouse.

I remember one trip from Las Vegas in the spring of 1991 where I chauffeured MT, Don King, and a journalist to Los Angeles. I heard King all wound up in the back of the limo so I decided to eavesdrop by way of the voice-activated intercom. "The Jew was the nigger of Germany," King said. King was into his rap about how "Hitler did to the Jews what the white man does to the black man in America." What the Nazis did was characterize the Jew as "evil" and a "cancer which had to be removed." And that's what "the system" in America did to the black people here by preaching "negrophobia," that blacks were "worthless and shiftless."

King claimed that the system was responsible for his being "held back" by the white man, even though the journalist quickly reminded him that he was the biggest name in boxing promotion and was about to close a business deal

153

worth more than $100 million. Don King dismissed that comment quickly and went on and on for what seemed like hours about the racism against blacks in this country, that the white man would never give the black man a fair chance to succeed. In the back of the limo, King had Mike Tyson as his captive audience for this incredibly repetitive rap. It was obvious that King was using on Tyson the same Nazi propaganda methods he had described to the journalist moments before: *creating belief through the use of constant repetition.*

At one point, the journalist jumped in and changed the topic to whether there was any truth to the allegations that over the years King had stolen huge amounts of money from his fighters. King insisted that it was just another example of racism that he be accused of such misconduct. His fighters, such as Muhammed Ali, Joe Frazier, Kenny Norton, Roberto Duran, never had accused him of taking their money. Only Larry Holmes had made such a charge but, King claimed, the press had overlooked Holmes' retraction of that allegation. Then he went on to say how many things he had done for Larry Holmes since the days when he didn't have a penny to his name before meeting Don King.

In late April of 1991, about a month after the first Tyson-Ruddock fight, Mike Tyson decided that he wanted to "see America" by driving cross-country in the black Lamborghini Diablo. MT sent bodyguard Anthony Pitts back to New York by plane as we headed east on the I-10 with me behind the wheel. I drove most of the the 3,000 mile journey while my boss did most of the snoring. Wherever we

154

went people recognized Mike Tyson. He enjoyed meeting them, shaking their hands, and handing out autographs. MT was not a snob nor thought himself too good for anybody. Fight fans were curious about the way the Razor Ruddock fight had ended, and Tyson was very concerned about the controversial decision. But what continued to bother him most was why he had to stand in line to have his day with Evander "Real Deal" Holyfield when there wasn't anybody else who should be ahead of him.

When we finally arrived in New York City, Tyson bought a new cobalt-blue Rolls Royce Silver Spur with a white interior and blue piping. We sent the Lamborghini for a much needed servicing. For a few days, we toured the City, including a stop at UltraSmith on West 38th Street in Manhattan. There Tyson had installed in the Rolls a 3,000 watt stereo system and headrest-mounted tvs like the units available on some airlines. The tvs were equipped with built-in Nintendo games which MT enjoyed playing as I chauffeured him around the City. There also were stops at the movies, restaurants, and familiar nighclubs. He kept returning to the same places, and to the same lady friends because, based on recent events, he now liked knowing what to expect. We also frequently visited his old Brownsville neighborhood.

When we stopped off at restaurants, I wouldn't sit with MT and his guests. Usually I would have the next table over shared with bodyguard Anthony Pitts. If MT was alone, then he might invite us to join him. We made sure that the waiter knew Tyson's drink should be served in a paper or plastic cup because he had a tendency to break glass with his vice-like grip. We also made sure that nobody approached his table without going through us first. Anthony's massive build and, if he wanted, menacing look, made people keep a respectful distance. Tyson had hired Anthony away from his bouncer job after he witnessed him pick up three guys at the same time and toss them out of an LA club.

One night during this period, when we were hanging out at the Marlborough House waiting for the start of training for Tyson-Ruddock II, MT walked into my bedroom wearing his lycra athletic shorts, the kind professional cyclists wear. Due to his unusually thick and muscular build, Mike Tyson could not wear regular underwear. He had been in his bedroom eating Chinese food with a girlfriend, but she had dozed off. Tyson sat on the floor and spread out a magazine.

"Rudy, I want to buy a bus. I want the *baddest* fucking bus you can buy. And I want it finished by the next Ruddock fight. Look into it for me, okay?"

The magazine was turned to a page showing a motor coach. But Tyson wanted to make something much bigger and better. He wanted to take another cross- country trip but with all the comforts of home.

"After the next fight, if Don King doesn't give me fucking Holyfield, then I'm not fighting for him no more."

The next morning I was on the phone to the publishers of the *Robb Report*, a magazine for the rich and famous. I wanted to find out who made the best motor coaches in the world. They directed me to a man named Louie Norman of the

Genesis company in Louisiana. The type of vehicle we were looking for never had been built. Without telling Norman whom I worked for, we made arrangements for him to come to New York. I picked him up at LaGuardia, and then we continued on to Rhode Island to the headquarters of the Hasbro toy company. During the trip, I revealed the name of the client and what he had in mind, and Louie Norman was fascinated with the idea. We sat down with four designers and told them about the very special motor coach we wanted to design and build. In less than four hours, the Hasbro people produced a drawing of a futuristic Genesis motor coach custom-built for Mike Tyson. It had two bedrooms and a one-car garage, a complete luxury condominium on wheels. There was a lot of excitement as we admired what the Hasbro people had come up with in such a short time. Louie Norman estimated that the vehicle alone would cost $600,000. I was assured that everyone would work around the clock to finish the Genesis motor coach by the deadline.

The next step was to have MT sit down with the Hasbro drawing and decide how he was going to furnish and equip the interior. We sat on the floor for five hours while he made his choices. There was going to be a lot of leather and marble and gold-plated fixtures, including the Roman tub. After we forwarded the final details to Genesis, we were told that the final sticker price was $1.3 million with an initial deposit of $1 million. That was fine with Tyson who ordered that fabrication commence immediately. Tyson instructed me to call Joseph Maffia, the comptroller at Don King Productions, and have him cut the deposit check.

Because I was going to have to pick up the check anyway, I decided to tell Maffia about it when I got there. After I explained why I was there, the people at the DKP offices freaked out. Don King wasn't there but was alerted about my presence and called to find out what was going on. Everybody wanted to know who had put this crazy idea into MT's head. Maffia finally informed me that he couldn't comply with the request. He told me that, if he issued a check for that amount, there wouldn't be funds sufficient to cover it. He also asked me not to relay that fact to MT but rather to do whatever I could to delay the Genesis project. I guess Joseph Maffia didn't know me very well. I worked for Mike Tyson, not Don King Productions, and was a stubbornly loyal servant. I didn't say so right then, but there was no way I was going to participate in this scheme. I departed DKP empty-handed.

When I returned to the Marlborough House, MT was sitting on the floor, his back leaning against the sofa, like he did most of the time. He was eating Captain Crunch out of the box while watching "Tom and Jerry" cartoons.

"Hey, man, did you get the check for the bus?"

I related everything that had happened at Don King Productions, including Joe Maffia's request that I delay the project and cooperate in the deception.

"Call the fucking office! I wanna' speak to that motherfucker personally."

Maffia must have told Tyson he would have to wait for

Don King to get an answer, which enraged MT, who was shouting angrily into the phone: "I want it now!" After a lot more yelling, MT finally agreed to wait a few days to pick up the check. That same evening Tyson had been looking through a real-estate publication and decided he wanted to purchase a larger apartment than the one he had at the Marlborough House. He told me to contact the company listing a certain property, Penthouse A in The Alfred Condominium, and set up a meeting. It looked like the apartment was going to be an $8 million cash deal. The lady real-estate agent from Brown Harris Stevens agreed to meet us at the DKP offices when we swung by there to pick up the Genesis deposit check.

On May 2, 1991, around noon, MT told me to take him to DKP to get his money for the motor coach. That day I was driving a Range Rover stretch limousine, a demonstrator, which Executive Coaches had loaned us. It was a fifteen-pack, twenty-five-feet long, with a plush white-leather interior, a 5,000 watt stereo system, and a rear compartment which was like a master bedroom. The Range Rover people wanted Tyson to try it out and see if he would purchase it for the modest price of $400,000. We showed up at DKP's three-story brownstone between Park and Madison without advance warning, the only person aware of our impending visit the lady real-estate agent from Brown Harris Stevens who was going to meet us there.

I parked the pearl-white limousine, which took up four spaces, and MT, along with me and Anthony, got out and climbed the steps to the front door of Don King Productions.

The receptionist buzzed us in. Once inside, I leaned over the counter and gave her a kiss as MT said he was taking the elevator upstairs to get his check. Tyson was on his way to the second floor where the executive offices were located. The real-estate agent arrived, and we sat in the lobby reviewing the information on the property MT was interested in. About five minutes had passed when the receptionist's intercom speaker crackled loudly, someone yelling that "a fight" had broken out upstairs. I recognized the voice as being that of Celia Tuckman, one of Don King's executives who was in charge of the pay-per-view portion of DKP's business affairs. Tuckman started screaming for the receptionist to call the police.

"Let's go!" I shouted to Anthony, and we bolted up the stairs.

I already had been to DKP enough times to be familiar with every detail of the layout. Although the legal dispute between Bill Cayton and DKP hadn't yet been resolved, and Cayton's contract officially didn't expire until February 12, 1992, Don King basically had taken over Tyson's career and personal affairs. Don King simply just started dealing directly with MT as if he already had won the battle for control, of course ably assisted every step of the way by King mercenaries John Horne and Rory Holloway.

I really didn't understand what was going on behind the scenes, and it wasn't my place to try and do so. For some time I had been going to the brownstone on 69th Street to pick up various items, including payroll checks for staff, hundreds of thousands of dollars of cash "expense money" for MT, and sealed envelopes containing paperwork for his

160

review.   These envelopes also would be sealed when I
returned them the next day to Don King Productions.   The
DKP offices also had been used to stage interviews and
promotional events.

Don King's office on the second floor had a desk crafted
in the shape of a crown, a conference table attached to it
around which a dozen people could sit.   Behind King's desk
there was a huge throne, done in a gold motif.   To the right
of the throne was a huge black and gold   safe, the old style
with the big "wheel" which King would spin to open its
heavy door, extracting large sums of cash he often handed
out.   There also were an array of monitors allowing King to
surveil every part of the premises, both inside and out.   There
were dozens of trophies and awards and scores of
photographs of Don King with famous people, including
Presidents Reagan and Bush, foreign political leaders, Michael
Jackson, and, of course, the professional fighters he had
promoted over the years, like Muhammed Ali.   There also
were large blowup posters relating to his career, reproductions
from magazine covers and articles.

The second floor contained three offices, those of
Joseph Maffia, Celia Tuckman, and Don King.   As we entered
King's office, we immediately noticed that Tyson's opponent
two months before, Razor Ruddock, was lying on the floor.
His hands were folded on his chest like he was on display
inside a coffin at a funeral home.   MT had knocked him out
cold, unlike the controversial technical knockout he was
awarded in the seventh round of the March 21 fight.   Don

King was behind his crown-shaped desk, his eyes bugging out in fear, as Tyson started climbing over the conference table to get to him.

We then noticed that there were two other people in the room. Seated on a sofa were two ogres known in the boxing business as "the twins" who worked as bodyguards for Razor Ruddock and his promoter, Murad Muhammed. One of the twins jumped up and tried to grab Tyson because he now had started advancing toward Don King. The other twin got into a fistfight with Anthony. Failing to reach MT, the first twin went for a bag. It looked to me like he was going for a weapon. This wasn't the right time to test my Aikido skills, the Japanese martial art which I recently had mastered to help me protect Mike Tyson. Instead, I pulled out my Glock 9mm semi-automatic and shouted "stop!" Then I glanced over at MT and saw him trying to isolate King behind his desk.

I turned back to the twin whose hand was still in the bag. "Get your fucking hand out of there!"

"I'll kill you!" Tyson shouted at Don King. "Why's this nigger here? What's he doing in my fucking building?"

King was babbling, insisting that Ruddock was there just to talk about the next fight.

"What fight? I'm not fighting that nigger! I want Holyfield!"

"Mike, goddammit, you better stop this shit! What the fuck are you talking about? Take it easy!"

"Where's my money? I want all my money now!"

Don King, seeing an opportunity, scurried out from behind his desk, out the door, and into the hallway. Tyson charged out after him.

"I've got these two guys," Anthony yelled over to me. "Get MT, don't let him do this!"

Don King was hiding out in Tuckman's office. By now most of the DKP staff had made their way to the second floor, trying to figure out what all the commotion was about. Tuckman was pleading with him to stop, but Tyson kept right on kicking and punching the walls, causing a number of pictures to fall to the ground. I came up to MT and told him to forget about Don King, that the cops were on their way. He didn't pay any attention so I grabbed his arm.

"Don't touch me, Rudy! Get the fuck off!"

I started pulling Tyson away from the door. Very angry, but very embarrassed at the same time by what he had done, MT gave in without a fight. We bolted down the stairs. By the time we reached the lobby, Ruddock, face bloody and still woozy from Tyson's punch, had made it down another staircase. He went for Tyson and they started struggling. Ruddock was no match for Tyson as MT began connecting with body punches to Ruddock's mid-section.

I was screaming at the receptionist to buzz us out, but she panicked and froze, so I produced the Glock 9mm and shot at the glass. As I opened the door for MT, he gave Ruddock a big roundhouse to the head which crumpled him to the floor like a rag doll. Outside, I aimed the keyless remote at the Range Rover limo which opened all the doors.

I pushed Tyson into the limo and locked all the doors to make sure Ruddock would not again reach him. We looked back for Anthony who was still inside. In a moment, he appeared at the front door, covered with blood, his face scratched from a big brawl with the twins. I lowered the front passenger window and yelled for him to get in. In the distance I could see Sarah Wallace from Eyewitness News, followed by cameramen, frantically making their way to the scene.

"Anthony!" I again yelled. "The media's here. Get the fuck in!"

Anthony was still at the front door when one of the twins appeared and tried to get into it again with him. Anthony spun around and planted a huge blow to his face, causing several of the twin's teeth to shoot out and onto the sidewalk.

There was a slight problem as Anthony piled into the front seat. There were cars parked in front and behind us which didn't leave me enough space to pull out. With no choice, I backed up, slammed into the car behind me, and pushed it back a few feet. Then I swung out and also hit another vehicle, a black Lincoln limousine, which had double-parked next to us. In so doing, I took off a good chunk of its front end. During this process, Sarah Wallace desperately was pursuing us, trying to get our attention, but I peeled rubber and we were gone in a flash.

Anthony wasn't in very good shape, and that further upset MT. It looked like one of the twins had bitten him badly on the hand. My first priority was to get Anthony a change because his clothes were covered with blood.

I parked in front of a sporting goods store on Madison Avenue, ran inside, and bought Anthony an extra-large sweatsuit and sneakers in record time, throwing money on the counter and not waiting for change. Anthony got into the new clothes in the back of the Range Rover limo, and I found a garbage can where I threw his blood-soaked clothes. He got back in front with me so MT could be alone. We talked about the events at the offices of Don King Productions. Anthony said that I had "done good" when I pulled out the Glock and trained it on one of the twins, and then when I had convinced Tyson to leave before he did something he probably later would regret. Anthony told me I had "kept a cool head" while everything had happened so quickly and violently.

MT was quiet for about twenty minutes during which time we drove around, waiting for further instructions. I finally lowered the partition and saw that he had dozed off so we just kept driving. After about an hour, both our Skypagers went off with messages to contact John Horne and Rory Holloway. Anthony got on the phone and called Horne. There was a lot of yelling back and forth. Finally, Horne demanded to know what Mike Tyson was doing, and Anthony hung up on him. MT woke up a few minutes later, lowered the partition, and stuck his head forward with a wide grin.

"You guys had my back. You guys are my niggers forever. Don't worry what happened there. You work for me." He reached for Anthony and gave him a hug.

"And, you, you crazy bastard," he said, squeezing my

head affectionately, "always looking for an excuse to protect me."

"You're not going to be happy with me, sir, because I smacked up the car."

"Don't worry about it, baby. I don't like it anyway."

We informed him about the pages from Horne and Holloway, and that they were looking for him.

"I don't wanna' talk to those niggers. Don King is gonna' pay for this!"

MT told us that he had been upset with Don King talking with Razor Ruddock behind his back. There apparently were a lot of unanswered questions why Ruddock and King needed to have that meeting without telling Tyson about it. After a few more minutes talking about what had happened, MT started joking about the incident. He laughed loudly when he recalled that Ruddock "had squealed like a pig." He also thought it was funny that he would end up buying the Range Rover, which he didn't really like, because it would cost too much to fix. We headed for the movies at 34th Street on the East Side where our boss wanted to see for the tenth time that year the original *Ninja Turtles* movie.

Later that afternoon on the five o'clock news, Sarah Wallace ran a piece on the fight at the offices of Don King Productions. She stated that a major incident had occurred there and displayed a napkin containing the teeth knocked out by Anthony Pitts which she had recovered on the sidewalk. She also showed the blood in front of the building. Later, a DKP official would deny that anything out of the ordinary had transpired that day.

If that were the case, why did Don King go out and purchase a bullet-proof vest that very same day?

It wasn't long after the fight at DKP before John Horne and Rory Holloway showed up to earn their keep by commencing the healing process between Tyson and Don King. They were smart enough to wait a couple of days while Tyson continued to cool down.   Then they appeared at the Marlborough House and tried to convince him that there was absolutely nothing wrong with what he had heard and seen at DKP a few days earlier. Horne and Holloway spent a lot of time talking about how dumb it would be to fight Evander Holyfield now because "the world was convinced that Razor Ruddock was *badder* than Holyfield." As usual, Horne and Holloway's incessant blabber got results. By the time they were through with him, MT was back on track for the next Ruddock fight.

Word got back to MT that Pope John Paul wanted to meet him. Once Tyson had travelled to Rome with Naomi Campbell, but the Pope found out too late about his presence in the Eternal City. A big Tyson fan, the Pope later extended an open invitation for a papal visit. Because MT was ripe at this moment for getting away from it all, he told me to contact the Vatican and make arrangements for us to fly to Rome.

Don King was getting very nervous with Tyson a continent away and out of the earshot of John Horne and Rory Holloway. Therefore, King rounded up his troupe and headed for Rome, arriving with Horne, Holloway, their wives, and DKP executive Celia Tuckman, where they started searching for us. After we had been located, King organized a trip to Warsaw, Poland for the entire group. Apparently, he had been relishing the day to see first-hand a piece of history which had been fascinating him for so long. Because we had nothing else to do, MT agreed to go along. King had chartered a private jet, and we all climbed aboard, destination Auschwitz. Apparently, King already had visited Dachau and other concentration camps on previous trips.

At Auschwitz, Don King was very animated, walking around touching everything. I already knew that Don King was an enthusiastic student of the Nazi movement and its propaganda techniques. I also knew that he possessed a collection of Nazi memorabilia. At his townhouse in mid-town Manhattan, I had seen display cases filled with swastikas and other items. At Auschwitz, Don King gathered up some of the earth and rocks and took them back to the States. Don King appeared fascinated every minute of his visit at the most gruesome death camp in the history of mankind.

I had only seen Mike Tyson cry twice during the more than four years I had known him by then. That was at the funerals of Jim Jacobs and Tyson's sister, Denise. Now, as Mike Tyson witnessed the crematoria at Auschwitz, and for the first time really understood what the Nazi concentration camps were all about, he could not hold back the tears.

In preparation for Tyson-Ruddock rematch on June 28, 1991, we reestablished our training camp in Las Vegas. However, this time we would not be living in a luxurious penthouse suite atop The Mirage. Steve Wynn had been extremely attentive to our needs. Every issue which had arisen had been quickly, effectively, and courteously resolved by Mr. Wynn and his very professional staff. At all times, they genuinely seemed to be proud to have us around the The Mirage. From our end, we had conducted ourselves properly and were not aware of any problems. That's why we were very surprised to learn from Don King that Mr. Wynn had told him he didn't want MT to stay at The Mirage anymore. Supposedly, we had given the hotel a bad reputation "running around there." I soon would discover that what Don King told us was an outrageous and vicious lie designed to distance MT from Steve Wynn, his gracious host and Tyson fight fan.

"The Mirage don't want no niggers running around there," King claimed. "So you niggers are going to use the house Mike bought in Vegas. You don't need to be hanging around those white people who don't want no niggers hanging around their places. And you," he added, staring at me. "You're just a nigger with straight hair."

King had arranged for Tyson to purchase a residence in the Las Vegas Country Club Estates. The residence, with six bedrooms, six bathrooms, a pool, gym, and gourmet kitchen, was next to a golf course behind the Hilton Hotel and was surrounded by a wall. I would have a room at a nearby motel, The Sheffield Inn, where I could crash, or use to entertain guests, during those sporadic, brief periods when I wasn't required to be with MT. Richard Giachetti, who took over Tyson's training after Kevin Rooney was fired, also was provided a room at that motel. He was a good and simple man, one of the best trainers in the business.

Tyson accepted what Don King told him, just as he had done so many times before. Using his mercenaries Horne and Holloway, King had an uncanny ability to erase almost any distrust or disgust which Tyson developed from time to time for "Daddy King." I remember the many hours we had spent, at King's insistence, watching those World War II documentaries, and how mass propaganda seemed to hypnotize the German people, making them zombie-like as they listened to their *Fuhrer. If somebody tells you something long enough, you will start to believe it.* And it didn't take a genius to figure out that's how Don King continued to hold Mike Tyson in his grip for so long. King's program was made even easier because Mike Tyson had a handicap about which I was not aware until a short time later. It was only then that I fully could understand why MT was so easily convinced by Horne and Holloway to do things against his best interests, and why his rages against King seemed to subside as quickly as they came.

Meanwhile, King, John Horne, Rory Holloway, and the DKP staff took up residence at The Mirage. Don King occupied that same luxurious penthouse suite which Steve Wynn graciously had provided MT while he prepared for the first Ruddock match. And Horne and Holloway were provided an adjoining suite. Now, getting ready for the Tyson-Ruddock rematch, Don King, using those same facilities for himself and his hired help, tried to keep MT away from the The Mirage as much as possible. King also took over space in The Mirage to run his business operations and brought in staff members, including Joseph Maffia, Celia Tuckman, and Gladys Rosa.

However, I would continue to go by the the hotel whenever I got a chance because I still had several girlfriends who worked there. That's how I learned that Don King' s explanation to us had been an outrageous and vicious lie designed to distance Tyson from Steve Wynn. My girlfriends all had been very surprised that we hadn't set up shop in the hotel just like before. They told me that Mr. Wynn, and everybody else at The Mirage, had been delighted to have us reside on the premises. Our presence had brought additional prestige and excitement to The Mirage's already super-charged atmosphere. Mike Tyson always was happy to shake hands with the hotel guests and handed out autographs wherever he might be. None of my girlfriends could recall a bad word being said about MT, Anthony Pitts, or me. The truth was that Don King believed Tyson was getting too chummy with Mr. Wynn. The Mirage already had shown an interest in promoting fights on its own before Don King ever had come into the picture. And with Tyson spending an extended period of time at the The Mirage, his luxury automobiles parked in front as if it were his own driveway, Don King was afraid that "his" fighter might find himself capable of having a direct relationship with a DKP competitor. The plan to have Don King and his intimates set themselves up in the sumptuous penthouse suite, and to keep Tyson stashed miles away a safe distance from The Mirage and Mr. Steve Wynn, was designed, engineered, and put into action exclusively by Don King.

Everything appeared to be going smoothly with less than a month to go before the fight. I was supervising the maintenance and organization of the house in the Country Club Estates. Tyson was training well under the very capable eye of Giachetti, and there was a lot of quiet time. Giachetti had set a strict training schedule, including a 7 p.m. curfew, so that Tyson would be rested and ready to arise at 5 a.m. for his daily six-mile jog before the desert sun came up. Giachetti mapped out a route which included some hills to increase Tyson's endurance.

There came a point in time where the spartan schedule imposed by Richard Giachetti finally became unbearable for MT who longed to visit some of his girlfriends in Los Angeles. As much as possible, my job was to be with Tyson twenty-four hours around the clock. When he was training, this meant also being his babysitter to make sure he didn't violate the special rules and curfews. And because Vegas had a great nightlife, nobody else wanted to help me out watching over him. Therefore, by the early evening, I usually was ready to hit the sack.

One night Tyson woke me up around 8 p.m. and told me he was going to sneak out and go to LA, a 385-mile six-hour drive, to see a girlfriend. I figured he was going to do it whether he had my blessing or not, and it would be safer if I went along. I pulled out the $750,000 Ferrari F40 Koenig which had a twelve-cylinder 1500 horsepower twin-turbocharged engine. It was nothing short of a rocket on wheels. Mindful that we would have to make the roundtrip in incredibly short time, we headed west at speeds up to 190 m.p.h. Tyson had spent many thousands of dollars for me to attend a race-car driving school in Phoenix where I qualified as a Formula 1 driver. I also had studied defensive and performance driving. MT loved speeding along the highway, and he got his money's worth that night. With the oversize super-wide rear tires, I was taking turns at 100 m.p.h. We made LA in less than 2-1/2 hours, Tyson saw his lady friend, and we were back at the Vegas house around 3.a.m. Incredibly, during our roundtrip we never encountered police or, if there had been any lying in wait, they decided there just was no way they were going to catch up to us.

Tyson had such a good time that first trip he snuck out he decided to risk it a few more times. The plan was for me to leave a note at around 8:00 p.m. at the front gate, that nobody was to enter the premises. I then would pull the Ferrari out, and Tyson would jump in, ducking down so Giachetti or anybody else spying on the house would think I was alone. If things went according to schedule, we would follow the same schedule, LA by 11 p.m., party until 1 a.m., and then back around 3.a.m. After sleeping only two hours, Tyson then would be roused by Giachetti at 5 a.m. for his early-morning six-mile jog. The human body, even Mike

Tyson's, has certain limits. It soon became apparent that something was wrong. Tyson was showing signs of weakness in the gym, and he was hobbling and wobbling more than jogging - He told everybody that he had been suffering from insomnia. Giachetti didn't buy it. One day he pulled me aside.

"Don't bullshit me, Rudy!" he snapped. "I had a look at the mufflers in that Ferrari."

I knew exactly what Giachetti was talking about. They must have looked like burnt marshmallows. At 190 m.p.h. hurtling across the Bonneville Salt Flats, the Ferrari Koenig spit fire. You could see the road behind us glowing red. Tyson's lead trainer was very concerned about being in top shape for the Ruddock rematch which was only a few weeks away. Since the days of Cus D'Amato, Tyson had been taught that one of the keys to being a top athlete is getting enough rest. Any partying was going to stop immediately and Tyson was going to be in bed sleeping by 8 p.m. Otherwise, Giachetti was going to fine me. I reported back to MT that our elaborate charade had been discovered, and that Giachetti was going to kick our asses if it happened again. Tyson agreed that he "better chill out" and called off the LA trip planned that evening.

I was going to take a night off since we weren't going to be up to any mischief. However, Anthony's fiance had come into town, as she would do on many weekends, so I decided to give them some time alone. Although Tyson said he was going to crash, there was something in his voice that made me suspicious. After awhile, lying on the living room sofa half-asleep in the pitch darkness, I thought ghosts were flying by me. When I finally focused my eyes, I realized it was a butt-naked Tyson with a black chick hurrying toward the staircase. Minutes later, there was some very loud moaning upstairs. I climbed the steps, opened the door to his bedroom, and poked my head inside. Although it was dark, I could make out the shapes of two bodies lying on the floor on the black sable "bedspread" which Tyson had purchased in Moscow.

"Hey, what's up?"

"Fuck, man. Just trying to get some sleep." Tyson thought I still didn't know about the girl.

"Sir, please do me a favor. When you've finished doing the *wild thing* with that black ghost next to you, please send her home so Giachetti doesn't dock my pay."

MT thought this comment was so funny that he rolled over and burst out into uncontrollable laughter. The next morning I went out and bought alarms for each door of the house. That night, I found myself again babysitting Tyson because everybody else already had plans. Because the door alarms were installed, at least I wasn't expecting a repeat of the previous night.

"You're not going to have any ghosts walking around again, are you?" I asked him out of caution anyway.

"Why don't you just take all those fucking door alarms, Rudy, and shove them up your motherfucking ass." Tyson laughed and went upstairs.

Finally I was getting some sleep when I heard a big

smack on the ground outside. I immediately hit the emergency switch which triggered lights all around the estate. Rushing outside, I ran into MT tangled up in a thorny bush. Trying to sneak out of the house without me knowing, Tyson had fallen from the second floor. If he hadn't been caught, he was going to roll the Ferrari silently down the driveway and onto the street to complete his getaway. I started helping him pluck the thorns out of his ass.

"Damn, I'm okay," he said in disgust waving me away. "Shit, man, I was gonna' get laid."

I started thinking, he's going to keep pulling this shit. If I'm not with him when he escapes, he'll probably get into worse trouble which is going to cost me, not just some money, but probably my job.

"Sir, if you're going to do this shit, at least take me with you. I work for you, not your career."

I made a big mistake by saying that. The next night we were back on the road to Los Angeles. Finally, about two weeks before Tyson-Ruddock II, Tyson finally realized that it was time to stop this craziness and concentrate only on the fight. The $750,000 Ferrari Koenig had a troubled history. It hadn't been designed for people like us but rather to be taken to the track once a month. But MT loved it so much he didn't care. We used to wear racing helmets because there was no top and, if bugs hit us at such high speeds, they could knock us out like a Tyson punch to the temple. Rick Black, of Black & Black Imports in Beverly Hills, did his best to assist us with servicing and repairing this vehicle. The Koenig had to be stripped down completely fairly often, just like a professional racing car after a major competition, which always cost a bundle. Then MT hit a speed bump too hard one day, causing damage to the front end. It took three weeks and $180,000 to get it back in shape. Another time, Tyson was showing off the car to a girlfriend and popped the clutch, snapping the driveshaft. This wasn't as hard to do as it sounded. The Koenig had three knobs, 500, 1000, or 1500 horsepower, and with a setting of 1500, the car literally jumped skyward from a dead stop. Rick Black was at the end of his rope with us and ordered a special titanium driveshaft which couldn't be broken except by nuclear fission.

Eventually, even MT got disgusted with the Koenig. He finally realized it wasn't practical and was costing too much to maintain and repair. But it was his pride and joy so I came up with a wild idea and had the car shipped to the Southington, Ohio estate. After Don King took over Mike Tyson's life, he convinced "his fighter" to buy a residence near his own in Ashtabula County just east of Cleveland. King owned 2,000 acres there and had built a thirty-room mansion complete with greenhouse and tennis courts and adorned with the American flag, another emblazoned with the word "Liberty," and a third with the Don King crown logo and the phrase "Only in America." King just happened to have the right property for Tyson in nearby Southington, 29,000 square feet under roof, including a massive game-room with a 5,000 watt stereo system. Anthony thought I had gone nuts when he learned about my scheme, and that I already had hired a contractor to knock a big hole in the gameroom's exterior walls without MT's permission.

"You're on your own!" said Anthony, not wanting any part of this "surprise" for MT. He was certain I'd be fired for this crazy idea.

One day, when Tyson returned to the Southington estate, he discovered the Ferrari F40 Koenig, mounted like a model airplane on a platform in the middle of the gameroom, and literally freaked out. He assumed that his favorite car had been sent to storage, and he'd never see it again.

"This is the *baddest* thing around!" he shouted when he first saw it, and I knew I still had a job.

"Just Sign Here"

On June 12, 1991, the temperature in Las Vegas was hovering around 115 degrees as we returned from the afternoon training session with Giachetti. With the countdown to the Ruddock rematch at just sixteen days, Tyson had buckled down. His pre-fight aggressiveness picking up, Tyson had knocked out three sparring partners that afternoon. He had committed himself to a fast track, to end the controversy about the first match by decisively crushing Ruddock this time around, and then taking on Holyfield to regain the championship crown. No one was going to delay this program, Don King and company included.

After driving back to the estate, I planned to jump into the pool with my clothes on. MT said he was going upstairs to take a shower, rest, and watch some cartoon videos. When he saw us enter the house, the new chef, Hans Strauss, started whipping up the protein shakes which Tyson would chug down by the pitcherful. Strauss, a four-star chef who had worked for a number of celebrities, had replaced Chef Early. Don King fired Chef Early allegedly for "sneaking out the back door with meat" from Tyson's residence. I never believed that bullshit excuse because Chef Early was a very honorable man. Tyson used to have a lot of fun with the tall, distinguished master cook of soul food, spending many hours shooting craps on the kitchen floor between meals. They had a deal that if Tyson won he would get some greasy food, like fried chicken or pork ribs, even if he was on his training diet. His presence was sorely missed by all of us, especially Mike Tyson.

Much later, sometime in 1993, I learned the real reason why Tyson's favorite chef and crap-shooting partner was dismissed by Don King. I was standing in a subway station in New York City wearing one of my "Team Tyson" leather jackets. A young black man approached me, saying he was a nephew of Chef Early. He gave me the telephone number for Chef Early Caterers on East Flatbush in Brooklyn. I called the next day and spoke with our old friend.

"I got fired 'cause I wouldn't put that `magic powder' in Mike's food," he told me.

I had no idea what the hell he was talking about, and Chef Early went on to tell me the shocking story. John Horne had given him a powder to be added to Tyson's food, supposedly an "endurance vitamin." Horne instructed Chef Early to keep this to himself because, although absolutely necessary to his training regimen, Tyson had been refusing to take it. Chef Early didn't like the explanation and didn't want to put anything extra into his boss' food without him or me knowing about it. Moreover, when he had a closer look at the "vitamin powder," he had found a tiny piece of an orange capsule with an "S" or "5." When Chef Early refused to follow Horne's instructions, Don King gave Tyson's favorite cook his walking papers.

Later, I checked with a pharmacy, mentioning that at one time Tyson had been taking Thorazine and Lithium. I was told that what Chef Early found in the powder could be part of a Thorazine capsule. The Physician's Desk Reference describes the Thorazine capsule as having an "opaque orange cap and natural body, imprinted "SKF" and either "T63," "T64," or "T66," depending on the dosage. Thorazine had been one of the anti-depressant medications administered to Mike Tyson after Roper and Givens had packed him off to the psychiatrist, the same psychiatrist who *later* agreed that Tyson wasn't suffering from any psychiatric disorder. It also was one of the drugs which Tyson had been taking the night of the infamous *"20/20"* interview where he had looked so sheepish and foolish in front of the camera. I later checked with a psychiatrist who told me that the drug would work like a sedative if administered to a person who didn't have a psychiatric problem. Someone easily could wonder why Chef Early didn't call Tyson after he was kicked out by Don King. The answer was simple. It wasn't easy to get in touch with us. Our phone numbers constantly were changing after Don King took over every aspect of Mike Tyson's career. Once, in a three-month period, they were changed six times by Don King Productions, supposedly for "our protection."

That June 12 afternoon, Hans Strauss mentioned to me that John Horne had left a large, sealed envelope on the long, black-marble dining-room table. As usual, I would give my boss these envelopes, which contained paperwork for his review, and then return the envelope to Don King Productions. Strauss told me that the envelope was to be sent back right away to the DKP offices at The Mirage. When I took the envelope upstairs, Tyson was on the phone, doodling on a pad, CDs and clothes all over the floor. He had been playing with one of his most important possessions, a miniature train set purchased after the first Ruddock fight. Costing $5,000, the train set fit into a steamer trunk which had built-in tracks, mountains, and tunnels. I dropped the big envelope on the bed and left. Taking off my clothes, I jumped in the pool for about a half-hour. When I got out and dried off, I ordered my favorite meal, barbecued seafood, from Chef Strauss. Just then, one of our Mexican maids marched toward me.

"I'm not going to do this job anymore, *senor* Rudy!" she said in very agitated Spanish. "He's an animal! He's throwing papers all over the room. I'm tired of always straightening up after him!"

Two of our other employees, another maid and the gardener, heard this commotion and came to the kitchen.

"Don't leave yet," I said, trying to calm her. "Let me see what's going on first."

I wasn't very happy about having my seafood barbecue interrupted by a Tyson temper tantrum. I also was surprised that MT was having one that afternoon because things had been pretty peaceful now that his training was in high gear for the Ruddock rematch. I bolted up the stairs, then slowly opened his bedroom door. Now, there wasn't just a mess of CDs and clothes all over the place, but also a lot of papers and checks and pieces of broken items. And while talking on the phone, Tyson continued flinging things around the room. Thinking about the big hassle of having to replace a good maid just because Tyson suddenly had gotten a bug up his ass, I lost control.

183

"What's going on!" I yelled at him, the first time I ever did since going to work for him. "I'm tired of you doing this shit! One of our maids just quit. Why are there papers all over the place?"

Tyson's eyes were wild as he suddenly lunged at me, grabbing my shirt and pulling me toward him. I hadn't expected this because he never had done anything like this in five years. Even though I knew Aikido, I was scared shit-less. Tyson could break me in two in a second if he wanted. I tried to relax, showing him that I wasn't going to resist.

"Rudy, I can't read, man," he said, his eyes watery. "Don is fucking macking me! All I do is keep signing. I'm tired of signing."

Since I met him in November of 1986, I never knew this about Mike Tyson. Then it hit me. At a fancy restaurant, Tyson would review the menu but end up saying "just order me whatever's best." He would look at newspapers, but only the "funny" section. And although I had seen him sign his name when he handed out autographs, the only other writings had been "doodlings."

"Don't worry about it. I'll read with you. I'll help you. Just calm down. We'll work it out together." I reassured him we'd find a way to understand all these checks and documents. "I'll pick this stuff up. Breaking shit ain't gonna' help."

At that point, he released me, and we sat down on the floor. I began gathering up all the checks and other documents that had been contained in the package delivered by John Horne earlier in the day. There were a lot of checks stapled to Don King Productions letterhead memos, and everything looked official. But as I started taking a closer look, I noticed that many checks had dollar amounts written in but otherwise were left blank. One of the checks which did have a payee was made out to "Centel," a cellular phone company in Las Vegas, in an amount over $100,000. I got very scared because that was my portable bill, the only person on Team Tyson who had a "flip-phone" from Centel. MT was going to think I had gone berserk calling my girlfriends for hours. But even if I had, it was impossible to spend more than $100,000 in only one month! Because there were no invoices attached to this check, only a memorandum stapled to it saying "just sign and return," I had no idea what calls were being charged. Tyson wanted to know what I was doing rummaging through all the documents.

"We've got to contact Joe Maffia, the comptroller at Don King Productions. We've got to demand invoices to know what you're paying. Like this Centel thing."

"That's our phones, right?"

"No way, man! We only have one phone. I don't want you to blame me for this huge bill. You don't have a $100,000 phone bill!"

Tyson was boiling. "Don King is stealing from me!"

By this time it was around 5 p.m. in New York, still time enough to catch Joe Maffia at DKP. There never had been any problem between Maffia and me during our frequent dealings. He always had been pleasant and courteous

185

whenever I needed to make arrangements for payment for MT's purchases. When he picked up the phone, Maffia seemed happy to hear from me.

"MT wants invoices for each item in the June package."

There was silence at the other end for a few moments.

"Rudy, what are you doing?"

"MT said there's checks for huge amounts of money and no invoices."

Again, there was a silence, but this time it was longer.

"My God, Rudy, what have you done?" he finally said in a cold, low voice.

"Joe, I'm standing in the bedroom with MT, and he wants me to take over the billing process starting now."

"I can't do nothing until I talk to Don." And with that, the line went dead.

MT got very agitated when Maffia hung up on us. The guy was his accountant, but Tyson couldn't get information on his own monthly expenses before first getting Don King's approval.

"Rudy, call that nigger back and put me on the phone."

When we called Don King Productions again, we were put on hold for several minutes.

"MT wants to talk to you," I told Maffia when he finally picked up and passed the phone to MT.

"If you don't want me to get on a plane and break your fucking face," Tyson barked, "fax what Rudy wants now, starting with the Centel bill!" Then he slammed down the receiver.

Mike Tyson looked over at me with an expression of relief, like a great weight had been taken off his shoulders. He was awakening from a deep, coma-like sleep. Tyson finally had someone who was going to help him get some answers to all the checks which had been shoved in his face for him to sign ever since Don King took over his affairs. And maybe he also looked relieved because he finally had confessed, to someone he trusted within his inner ring, that he couldn't read. I always had assumed that MT read and understood the contents in all those sealed envelopes delivered to him, and then returned by hand to Don King Productions, mostly by John Horne. After all, MT was President of his own corporation, Mike Tyson Productions. But now I realized that he had been living with a painful, silent handicap for a very long time. And it was this handicap, which he had been too embarrassed to admit, that had given others a blank check to mislead and deceive and commit fraud upon Mike Tyson.

It only took a few minutes before the fax beeped, announcing that documents were on their way from New York. By then, I had looked at a lot more checks. I was stunned to find that Mike Tyson was being billed for living and training in his own camp. There was a check made out from Mike Tyson Productions to Don King Productions for $300,000, the notation on the line in the lower-left-hand corner "living expenses." How could Mike Tyson be paying $300,000 to live in a residence he already supposedly owned outright? It got much worse. There were other checks issued by Mike Tyson Productions. To Don King's daughter for $52,000, salary for being Vice-President of "The Mike Tyson Fan Club." Another to Henrietta King for consulting fees in the amount of $100,000, although she never did anything for Mike Tyson. In fact, King family members rarely even took the time to say hello to Mike Tyson when they happened to be around. And then there were the John Horne and Rory Holloway checks, $400,000 *each.* The "memo lines" on these checks contained a simple line through them as if to say "nothing in particular."

As the fax machine kept spitting out the invoice from Centel, I began to carefully review the long invoice. Mike Tyson was being billed for the cellular phones and Skypagers of the entire staff of Don King Productions and also for members of Don King's family and others who had no affiliation whatsoever to Mike Tyson Productions. Joseph Maffia, comptroller, #8223813. Carl King, Don King's son, #292886. John Horne, #73929. Rory Holloway, #8223817. Coylette James, Don

King's secretary, #8223810. Dana Jameson, executive assistant, #8223811. Gladys Rosa, Latin representative, #8223812. Greg Lee, Don King's son-in-law, #1459. James Cassidy, Don King's son-in-law, #14597. Jerome Jordan, Don King's bodyguard, #13670. Joe Safety, DKP media director, #2221796. Todd Holloway, Rory Holloway's brother, #8223819. Coy Sparks, DKP in-house courier, #8223814. Isadore Bolton, Don King's butler, #8223818. Captain Joe, Don King's chauffeur, #49021. Only three names should have appeared on that bill, Mike Tyson, Anthony Pitts, and Rudy Gonzalez, because we were the only persons who worked for Mike Tyson Productions.

Sitting there surrounded by this mound of papers and checks, we realized that Mike Tyson Productions, in the month of June, 1991 alone, was about to shell out nearly $1.5 million in expenses which shouldn't have been billed to it at all. The professional boxer pays his manager a percentage of his gross revenue and, in exchange, the manager has to perform certain services at his own expense. The fighter doesn't pay *twice.* And the fight promoter gets a percentage of fight revenue, an amount which is controlled by professional boxing regulators. If the promoter has a company and staff, he pays them out of his own revenue. Otherwise, the boxer ends up paying *twice.* I remembered the times when Tyson would meet with his former co-managers, Jim Jacobs and Bill Cayton, and they would sit with him and explain in detail what was being spent and why. With them, there had been receipts and formalities. With Don King, Mike Tyson simply had become a blank check.

We sat on the floor going over the checks and documents for what seemed like hours. In fact, only a few minutes had passed. We discovered three more expenses which never should have been billed to Mike Tyson Productions. Checks had been prepared by Don King Productions for Mike Tyson to sign which related to rental of three New York apartments. They were in the names of Celia Tuckman and two other Don King Production employees. One apartment alone cost $12,000 per month, another $8,000. While we were reviewing these rental expenses, and only about twenty minutes after the fax had started rolling along, we heard a big commotion downstairs. A moment later, like a runaway train, Don King and John Horne stormed into the bedroom. Obviously, someone had made them aware of our transcontinental demand for documentation.

Mike Tyson jumped up and shook a finger at Don King. "I'm through with you, motherfucker! You've been stealing my money!"

King glared in my direction. "Don't listen to this fucking kid!"

"No, he's not lying. He just sat down and been reading with me all this shit I been signing. Why am I paying your family?"

With that, Tyson started grabbing anything in sight and went on a smashing rampage. Then he wheeled around and knocked John Horne to the ground.

"You've known about this shit!" He screamed at Horne who lay in a silent heap, waiting for "Daddy King" to resolve the crisis as he always had done before.

"Go downstairs, motherfucker," said King, cocking his head toward me.

191

As I turned to leave, Mike Tyson disappeared inside the bathroom and slammed the door. I headed downstairs and noticed the curious staff gathered below. Outside, I sat on the black Diablo parked in the driveway. Suddenly, I got very scared about what I had started less than an hour before. There had been rumblings for some time about Don King's ripoffs of other fighters such as Muhammed Ali and Larry Holmes. We had been experiencing our own whispers from the darkness of the kingdom, like that day we had arrived unannounced at Don King Productions to pick up the Genesis deposit. We still didn't have the check more than three weeks later. After a few minutes, John Horne exited the house and quietly ordered me to go to my room at the Shieffield Inn and await further instructions.

"I don't want to look at you anymore," Horne added.

I opened the door to the Diablo and started to climb in.

"Give me the keys. You can't use the Lamborghini. Mike doesn't want anybody using his cars."

"Fuck you, John Horne!" And with that, I fired up the Diablo, laid rubber, and kicked dirt and gravel behind me and into Horne's face.

If I had stayed a moment longer, I knew I was going to severely kick the ass of that fucking weasel John Horne. At the Sheffield, I took a shower and changed my clothes. Anthony called me a few minutes later.

"Yo, what did you do, man? You brought down the house." Apparently, Anthony had walked into the house a few moments after I left. "MT wants to talk to you."

192

"What are you doing in your hotel room?"

"I'm sorry, sir. John Horne told me to come here. I'm sorry for everything."

"Don't apologize, Rudy. Take the rest of the afternoon off. I'm throwing Anthony out too. I wanna' think this over. Call me tomorrow. I wanna' be alone now."

That night I took the Diablo and hit downtown Vegas. I swung by The Mirage and picked up one of my girlfriends, Candy, a blackjack dealer originally from Bogota, Colombia. We drove to Boulder City, about twenty-five miles southeast of Vegas. When we got back, she spent the night. The following morning I returned to the house to assess the damage. It was a wreck, in much worse shape than I had left it. I knew I was going to have a long day reorganizing the place.

We didn't hear a peep from Don King, John Horne, or Rory Holloway for several days. Things went back to "normal" as MT continued to train rigorously with Richard Giachetti. I could tell by his manner that my boss felt much closer to me after what had transpired on June 12.

"I'm either gonna' fight Holyfield or retire, Rudy. I'm tired of the abuse."

A few days before, I had visited The Sharper Image in downtown Vegas. There I purchased a pocket-size photocopier manufactured by Panasonic which you can hold in your hand and "scan" any document you want to reproduce.

On the evening of June 18, 1991, Anthony took the graveyard shift, 9 p.m. to 6 a.m. Again, I was driving the Lamborghini Diablo because earlier I had been busy detailing it and getting it back into mint condition. With Anthony babysitting Tyson that night, I decided to sleep in my room at the Sheffield. I picked up Vanessa, a Miami Cuban who worked one of the crap tables at The Mirage, and partied with her all night. Around 8 a.m. the next morning I was in a deep sleep when the cellular phone rang. It was Dana Jameson, Don King's executive assistant.

"Rudy, Don wants you to go pick up his new Bentley coupe in LA and bring it here. Captain Joe is sick. And he's taking medication so he can't drive. Don knows you're a good driver and won't smash up his new car."

Until that day, I had never been asked to run any errands for Don King. As far as I was concerned, I only had one master and his name was Mike Tyson. I informed Jameson that if MT wanted me to run this errand, then fine. She suggested that I stop reporting to Mike Tyson.

"Rudy, you still don't get it, do you? Everybody works for Don King. Even Mike. So why don't you just do what we tell you to do and stop creating problems?"

I wasn't going anywhere without MT's permission and went back to sleep. An hour later, the hotel phone rang. It was John Horne.

"Why aren't you up yet? You're supposed to be ready to go to LA. And I also want you to pick up two jackets for Whitney Houston and her mom and take them to Jeff Hamilton."

Horne explained that the singer was in town performing, and she also was going to attend the Tyson-Ruddock rematch. Apparently, Houston's mother owned a home in

Las Vegas. There had been problems with their Jeff Hamilton leather jackets, Houston's was the wrong size, her mother's had an error in the spelling of her name. I told him the same thing I had said to Dana Jameson.

"Rudy, I'm here with MT right now. Now get the fuck on a plane and go to fucking LA right now and do what you're told to do!"

I got Vanessa out of bed, we dressed, and ran out the door. Because I wasn't about to leave a $450,000 Tyson automobile in the airport parking lot, I had to return to the house. I paged Anthony who responded by walkie talkie, a communication system we also used which had about a ten-mile range.

"I need you to take me to the airport. I can't leave the Diablo there. Meet me at the house right away."

By the time I arrived, Anthony's yellow Corvette already was in the driveway. We had rented three Corvettes from Vegas' Rent-A-Vet, and I also always had the exclusive use of one of them. I opened the front door, expecting to find MT. Instead, John Horne was sitting in the living room, a look of shock coming over his face.

"What are you doing here? You're supposed to be in LA!"

"Where's MT?"

"Upstairs sleeping. Don't bother him. Go get Don King's car now. He needs it right away!"

Anthony took me to pick up the Whitney Houston jackets and got me to McCarran International in time to grab an 11:00 a.m. flight to LA. Anthony and I had become good friends, having spent so much time together over the past few years, like a marriage without sex. We would give our lives for each other. We had a simple code of honor which bound us together, *"safe passage for Mike Tyson."*

I did two things that morning before I left Vegas. First, I normally would have taken the Lamborghini's keys with me. But that day, when nobody was looking, I stuck them in a cookie jar. I also placed a call to an old girlfriend, Daisy, an ex- stripper who lived in LA. I told her to pick me up at the airport so I wouldn't have to hassle with arrangements to get around town. She agreed in exchange for a promise of wild sex. Those two things, I soon found out, would save my life later that day.

"Final Errands"

After the forty minute flight to Los Angeles, I was met by my lady friend, Daisy, who was waiting for me at the gate. The former stripper was in her late forties but was looking great. We had met a few months before on a connecting flight to LA and, at that time I didn't know that Daisy was related in some way to Gladys Rosa, a Don King Productions executive. We jumped into Daisy's Mustang and headed for the LAX Holiday Inn where we stayed for three hours. After that, we continued on to Tyson's apartment on Wilshire Boulevard where I needed to retrieve a diamond Rolex and two bags of Gianni Versace clothing. I instructed Daisy to park the Mustang in the garage and wait for me in the lobby. Because it was a sunny day, we walked north on Wilshire Boulevard to the Rolls Royce dealership of Beverly Hills.

Dressed in a two-piece Versace silk pajama-suit, I looked the part of someone who just had purchased a very expensive luxury automobile. Don King had ordered a canary-yellow Bentley Continental R, a two-seat roadster with white interior, yellow piping, and gold steering wheel bearing the Don King Enterprises crown logo in its center. The Bentley also had gold crown logos on the doors, and the paint job was so beautiful you wanted to lick it. The hood ornament was encrusted with diamonds. Obviously, this was not the kind of vehicle you could ever leave on the street unattended. There had been talk that Don King was going to design special-edition luxury automobiles and sell the idea to Rolls Royce.

After the paperwork was completed, I drove the

Bentley across the street to the Lamborghini dealership. We didn't have the Bentley's top down because it was too hot outside and needed to run the A/C. Later on we were going to put it down on the open road to Vegas. The Lamborghini people now had the custom-fitted luggage which came with Tyson's Diablo but which hadn't been ready when we took original delivery. After retrieving these pieces, we continued heading southwest toward Jeff Hamilton's factory. Back in 1987, I had heard about Jeff Hamilton, that he made leather jackets for celebrities ranging in price from $5,000 to $100,000. In 1983 Jeff Hamilton had become famous as the founder of "Guess Jeans for Men." In 1989, I met Jeff for the first time when MT had me fitted for five jackets with matching pants. MT didn't want me wearing a regular chauffeur's uniform. Instead, he wanted to have the *baddest-looking* chauffeur around. Over the years, I have continued to maintain my friendship with Jeff Hamilton. Although very well-known and very wealthy, Jeff always has been extremely considerate and sincere, a refreshing contrast to most celebrities. There have been many "copycats" who have tried to imitate Jeff Hamilton's craftsmanship. But there is only one Jeff Hamilton who continues to produce his unique creations in his present company, Jeff Hamilton Industries, located in LA.

Daisy and I were peppering romantic talk with dirty jokes as the traffic inched along. Suddenly, my Skypager went off, logging in the number for Don King Productions in Las Vegas. At the end of the number was the message "911-911," meaning "call immediately!" I made several attempts on my cellular "flip-phone" but couldn't get through to a "roaming" operator. Although the Bentley had a built-in phone, it hadn't yet been activated. Seconds later I got another page exactly like the first. Now I was getting concerned about calling the office right away, especially in light of what had been happening the past few days. And there I was stuck in a classic LA traffic jam without immediate phone access.

I turned right onto Beverly Hills Drive, going in the direction of Pico Boulevard. I spotted a carwash at the corner, pulled up to a bank of three pay phones, and parked. I climbed out and walked five feet to the phones and, using my long-distance calling card, dialed the number for Don King Productions at The Mirage Hotel. Dana Jameson answered.

"Why is John Horne fucking beeping me `911-911'? I've already picked up Don King's Bentley."

"I didn't page you, Rudy, " she said defensively. "And I'm the only one in the office. Everybody's out at MT's house."

I was pissed about being delayed on my way to see Jeff Hamilton. "If anybody calls, tell them I'm on my way back to Vegas. I already picked up a few things for MT."

"No problem," said Jameson.

I hung up and dialed Jeff Hamilton Industries. Jeff was out of the office attending an NBA playoff game, but he had alerted his staff to be ready to accommodate me and repair the Whitney Houston jackets.

"We'll fix things up for you no matter how long it

199

takes," his secretary told me.

I hung up and started walking back to the Bentley. On my right side, I noticed the presence of a short young black male about five yards away.

"Yo, mister, that's a *bad* car you got there!"

"Thanks," I said as I kept walking, the keys to the Bentley in my hand. I was a step away from getting back into the car when he shouted out again.

"Yo, man!"

I turned sideways to see what the deal was and noticed that the guy had advanced to about six feet away from me. He also had a snubnose 38-caliber handgun trained on my head. There were a few beats of silence. The gunman hadn't asked for my wallet or jewelry or even the keys to the $300,000 automobile. I knew then he was just going to shoot me for no reason. Out of fear or training, or both, I did whatever I could to protect my head, ducking and covering it with my elbow. At that instant, the assailant started firing. The first bullet entered my elbow as I started lunging toward the shooter. The second bullet tore through the bicep muscle. Both shots drove me back against the driver's side door. One of the arteries had been destroyed by these two shots, and blood was spurting from it like a high-pressure hose. Losing all control of my arm, it now hung limply at my side.

Daisy was hysterical inside the Bentley as my blood spattered against the driver's side window like wind-driven red rain. I wasn't feeling pain yet. Instead, the sensation I had was that everything around me was happening in slow motion. As I hit the door I spun around and heard another shot, this one striking me in the upper groin, ricochetting off my dragon-shaped beltbuckle, finally lodging itself in the thick Versace leather. If it weren't for the beltbuckle, the third bullet would have ripped open my stomach. I began to lose consciousness and slid slowly down the side of the door until I was sitting on the ground. In the distance, I could see my attacker running away.

My brain screamed at me "Don't stay there!" I struggled to a crouching position and opened the door. Daisy was still hysterical and, now inside, I was spraying her all over with blood from my torn artery. Somehow I managed to start the car and take off. The next thing I remembered was a man in a station wagon yelling at us, indicating where there was a hospital nearby. Realizing that I was fading fast, Daisy got me to stop the car, then jumped out and ran around to the driver's side. She pushed me over and got behind the wheel. By now, Daisy's face was completely covered with blood as she sped toward the hospital.

It was very bizarre because, from the moment I took the first shot, I never felt any pain. Rather, a peaceful feeling was spreading throughout my body, like I had been injected with a very strong tranquilizer. Everything kept slowing down so much that, as my eyes finally closed, there was only the click-click of frozen frames. Daisy screamed that we were finally at the hospital. I got out to walk to the emergency entrance and immediately experienced a big white flash and was on the ground. Four paramedics rushed out, asking me questions I could not understand. I made out two police uniforms. Then somebody was cutting my pants off, and I kept babbling "why are you doing that?"

"We're gonna' lose him!" one of the paramedics kept shouting.

Daisy was nearby, screaming over and over "Don't close your eyes!"

One of the police officers said: "Did you get a load of that car?"

The other cop was looking down at me: "What did you do?"

The paramedics lifted me onto a stretcher and began rolling me toward the emergency entrance.

"Keep still," one of them said to me. "You've lost a lot of blood."

In a few moments I was in the operating room, the strong smell of antiseptic filling my nostrils.

A doctor covered by a face mask was hovering over me: "You're hemorrhaging and have lost a lot of blood. We're going to put you out. Is there anybody you need to call?" I just wanted to close my eyes. I had no strength, not even to speak one word. Sleep, that's all I wanted. I began a dream where I was lost inside a big castle, wandering through the long hallways, wanting to enter and sleep in each room.

It was a very relaxing, cozy dream. Finally, in a low voice, I heard my name being called. It seemed like the dream had been only a few minutes. In fact, I had been out for hours. After hearing my name being repeated several times, I finally opened my eyes. Anthony Pitts was standing over me.

"Are you okay?"

"He didn't try to rob me. I have all MT's stuff."

"Man, what are you thinking? You've been shot." Anthony was shaking his head because I had my priorities pretty fucked up. "Hey," he added. "There's somebody here to see you."

As he approached the side of my bed dressed in sweat-pants and a jacket, Mike Tyson looked disoriented.

"I found the keys, Rudy," he said softly. MT was talking about the keys to the Diablo which I had left back at the house before Anthony took me to the airport. Sometime ago I had mentioned to MT, that if I wasn't going to be around for awhile, I would leave the keys to the cars in a place he wouldn't easily forget, the cookie jar in the kitchen where he always was poking around anyway. Shortly after midnight, when they heard about what happened to me, he and Anthony bolted out of the house, grabbed the Diablo, and raced across the desert to be by my side at the hospital in Los Angeles.

"I didn't do nothing wrong. He didn't take anything."

"Don't concern yourself with that." MT glanced over at Anthony like "why is he still talking about my stuff when he almost just got killed?"

Out of the corner of my eye I could see that Tyson's

expression was both sad and scared. "You know they're trying to kill you, right?" He gazed at me in silence for a few moments. "I don't want them to operate on you here. I want you to go to Vegas. I want you to go straight to the house in Vegas."

Our conversation was over because I passed out, for what seemed like only a minute, but in fact was several hours. As daylight streamed through the window in my room, I experienced massive pain throughout my body, even in my toes. My back and shoulders felt like somebody was sticking needles in them. As I lay there waiting for a doctor or nurse, I had no idea whether I was going to be crippled as a result of any of the injuries I sustained in the shooting. Anthony was trying to make arrangements to get me released but was encountering resistance. Finally, against the attending physician's advice, and after taking care of the forms releasing the hospital from any liability, Anthony checked me out. During my operation, the doctors had fitted me with an artificial artery. Wrapped in bandages, still bleeding and in massive pain, Anthony shuttled me to the airport where we caught a plane to Vegas. MT had made arrangements for me to be admitted to the hospital, but first Anthony told the cab driver to take us to the house. When we got there, Anthony opened the door for me. Inside I saw Don King, Rory Holloway and John Horne and their wives, and my boss. MT walked up to me slowly.

"Are you okay?" Tyson said, a glazed look on his face like he had been drugged.

King, Horne, and Holloway turned around and were

obviously shocked to see me standing there.

"What were you doing with my Rolls? What were you doing in California?"

Don King denied he told Dana Jameson to send me on the errand to pick up the Bentley. Tyson was staring at Don King and Rory Holloway. John Horne had turned so that Tyson wouldn't be able to see his face.

"You're stupid!" Horne said to me. "You should've given up the car. Why did you get shot up? It had insurance."

Before I could respond, MT fixed his gaze on Horne. "They didn't wanna' rob him. He didn't get shot at over that. Why don't you stop playing games? You niggers are trying to kill him because of the checks."

There was a stunned silence in the room. They all looked at MT like he had made the joke of the century and started chuckling. But Tyson's expression remained dead serious. Then MT told Anthony to take me to Lake Meade Hospital Medical Center. When we arrived, the doctors were standing by so surgery could be performed right away. I had a second surgery that same week. For a time, there was concern that the path created by the bullet might paralyze my arm from the elbow down. I refused to accept that, going over and over in my mind that I would be okay. I was very fortunate and eventually regained most of the mobility in the arm ripped apart by the gunshots.

Because I needed absolute rest during my recuperation, I wasn't able to attend the Tyson-Ruddock "rematch" on June 28, 1991, which, just like the first fight, was held in the outdoor arena of The Mirage Hotel.

I watched the Tyson-Ruddock bout on TV from my hospital room. For the first time in four years, Mike Tyson was forced to go the entire distance in a fight before winning by a decision. The last time had been on March 7, 1987, when he won by a decision against "Bonecrusher" Smith at the Las Vegas Hilton. Tyson's punches were good enough to break a bone in Ruddock's jaw, but not good enough to knock him out in traditional early-finish Tyson style. In fact, as MT struggled to put Ruddock away, the crowd turned on him and began cheering the embattled Ruddock in the closing rounds. Although Tyson's record was now 41-1-0 with thirty-six knockouts, he still wasn't heavyweight champion. Tyson could only accomplish that objective at this point in time by fighting Evander Holyfield, something he had been insisting on for months. And now everybody was waiting, with the Ruddock controversy put to rest, for that date finally to be set. Don King immediately tried to sandbag that from happening as soon as Tyson-Ruddock II ended. "He has proven he is bigger than the title! He is bigger than any fighter in the world. You're talking about a symbol." By this, of course, Don King meant that there just wasn't any reason for Tyson to fight Holyfield because the heavyweight title was just ceremonial.

"You wonder how long King can continue selling this frayed bill of goods to Tyson," reported the *Los Angeles Daily News* two days after the fight. "You wonder how King can keep Tyson focused on the Nov. 1 fight with Foreman he is proposing. You wonder when Tyson will end the charade, look King in the eye and say enough is enough: My next fight will be with Holyfield for the title and it will take place with or without you. You wonder if King is scared to death."

Dan Duva, Holyfield's promoter, offered Tyson $15 million for a chance at the title. King responded by claiming Duva was imposing terms which weren't favorable enough to make a deal, and that he wanted $25 million for Tyson. King also said that Duva had demanded options for future Tyson fights on Holyfield's pay-per-view network, TVKO. However, TVKO's President, Seth Abraham, denied that such a demand had been made a condition for setting up the Tyson-Holyfield fight. "There are two opponents out there we want, Holyfield and Foreman," said Don King, "and the way things are now, whichever one signs first with us will be the one we go with." King offered Foreman $15 million plus a percentage of pay-per-view on KingVision if he would fight Tyson on November 1, 1991 at The Mirage. "King doesn't want Tyson to fight Holyfield," said Dan Duva, "because if Tyson loses, King won't have any influence in the heavyweight division."

Shortly after I was released from the Lake Meade Hospital Medical Center, I was informed by Don King's secretary that there were two detectives from the L.A.P.D. who wanted to question me and show me photos of suspects in my shooting. I didn't recognize any of the photos shown to me. The detectives said they would get in touch with me again but never did.

The day after the Tyson-Ruddock rematch, MT asked me to return with him to The Big House in Southington,

Ohio, located about 80 miles east of Cleveland in Amish country. MT spent most of his time there just hanging out doing nothing. He still was waiting, his impatience growing to fever pitch, for Don King to set up the Evander Holyfield bout. Mike Tyson was determined to be world heavyweight champion by the end of 1991, whether Don King agreed or *not*. In fact, Tyson already had been out of control for some time, a loose cannon, doing things on his own which had been pissing Don King off to no end. For example, on December 28, 1990, about eleven months after the Buster Douglas fiasco, Tyson filed a $50 million lawsuit to stop the heavyweight match between Holyfield and George Foreman, scheduled for April 19, 1991 in Atlantic City. The suit was filed in the U.S. District Court for the Southern District of New York against the World Boxing Association and the International Boxing Federation. The other major boxing organization, the World Boxing Council, had ruled that Tyson should fight Holyfield for the title. Tyson alleged in his complaint that he should have been allowed to fight Holyfield, the winner against Douglas in a fight held two months before at The Mirage. He also stated that Holyfield wanted to fight Foreman because he would be easier to beat.

The relief Tyson was seeking in that legal action directly conflicted with King's game plan for staging a series of Tyson "road to recovery" matches designed to rake in millions for Don King Productions. By July, 1991, there already had been four such "recovery" fights, Tillman, Stewart, and Ruddock twice. For Tyson, all this posturing made absolutely no sense.

This was *not* about money. It was about deciding who was the *best* heavyweight fighter in the world. And in July, 1991, just as it had been in December, 1990, that issue only could be decided by Tyson fighting the current heavyweight title-holder, Evander "Real Deal" Holyfield. It made no difference to Tyson whether that fight would be held at Caesar's Palace or in an alley down the street.

Mike Tyson was still waiting for Don King to provide him answers about his financial situation and what had happened to me in Los Angeles. None had yet been provided to Tyson about the Genesis coach and the money that Mike Tyson Productions was paying for Don King Production expenses. Tyson also had given the word, John Horne and Rory Holloway were not to be around him constantly like they had been ever since Don King had taken over his business affairs. There always had been girls around Mike Tyson because he had an incredible sexual appetite. But during these days after the Ruddock rematch, Tyson spent more quiet time dwelling on what had been happening in his life these past few weeks. He did have some local girlfriends swing by from time to time, but he spent more time watching cartoons and ninja movies. On the night of July 17, 1991, Tyson was sleeping upstairs after entertaining a few friends who were visiting from LA. I answered the phone around midnight. It was the mother of Demencio, one of Tyson's close childhood friends from the old neighborhood in Brooklyn, calling from Washington, D.C. where Demencio's family had moved sometime back. Demencio always had kept in close touch with MT over the years and had attended most of his fights. Demencio's mother informed me that her son had been shot to death earlier that day. The reason for the killing was still a mystery. I went upstairs and told my boss about the death of his friend. Tyson picked up the phone and began consoling Demencio's mother. I went back downstairs.

A few minutes later, MT descended, very upset, and walked past me toward the garage. I heard the roar of the Porsche Speedster, the fastest automobile in Tyson's collection, heading down the driveway. The security guard called and asked what to do. I said "open the gates!" I got on the phone to Ouie in New York who was Demencio's friend.

"Lock down the house, Rudy," Ouie told me. "Go after MT. Don't let him go to D.C. There might be some type of war going on there. And they might retaliate against MT."

I quickly rounded up the staff and told them to leave immediately because we were shutting down the house. Only Maria, our current chef, was to remain at the Southington estate.

By the time I got everything organized and could leave, Tyson had more than an hour's jump on me. I grabbed a few personal items, tossed them in the black Ferrari Testarossa and headed east on I-80, driving like a maniac in search of Tyson. Somewhere in Pennsylvania I saw Tyson in the distance being chased by the highway patrol. I was clocking Tyson at that time doing about 160 m.p.h. I didn't want to lose them, but I didn't want to get stopped either so I slowed down. A few minutes later I was able to reach Tyson because he finally had been pulled over by the troopers. They were about to arrest him when I approached one of the troopers, a towering black man. I identified myself as Mike Tyson's bodyguard and mentioned that I had been trying to catch up with him. I told the trooper that one of Tyson's best friends had been killed in D.C., that he was very emotional and upset, and that he was trying to get there to find out what had happened. The trooper let me know that he had to give Tyson a ticket because it already had printed out, but he was understanding and agreed not to arrest him. However, Tyson would receive a ticket for speeding and also would have to leave the Porsche at a nearby service station and continue on with me. The trooper considered Tyson a menace to himself and others in that emotional state and escorted us to the service station to make sure we followed his orders.

After we parked and locked the Porsche, Tyson jumped in the Testarossa, and we headed for D.C. It was an eight-hour drive but we did it in four, arriving around six in the morning. Once in the Capitol, we went to the apartment of a long-standing Tyson girlfriend, Sherry Brown, located in a poor section of town. I stayed with the car while MT went inside. During the entire trip Tyson had been very upset and agitated. I was so exhausted that I fell asleep, awakened sometime later by my Skypager, the number logged in that of the house in Southington. Glancing at my watch, I realized now it was nearly 9 a.m. I called the number expecting the chef to answer. Instead, Don King's voice came over the line.

"Goddammit, where's Mike?" King demanded to know. "Where are you fucking guys now! I need to talk to Mike."

"DK, one of his friends got killed last night. We just got into D.C. this morning and he's upstairs sleeping in Sherry's apartment."

"I've gotta' talk to that nigger right now!"

"Sir, I'll give him the message," I said and hung up.

After locking the car, I went inside Sherry Brown's building to speak with MT and found him passed out on the couch. I placed my hand on his shoulder in a special way which was a sign to him that it was me. "Hey, boss." You just didn't tap Tyson on the arm or head because he could wake up swinging. For this reason, I was the only one who ever woke him up. Even Robin Givens used to tell me to wake her husband up. It was too dangerous.

"Don King wants to talk to you."

"I don't wanna' talk to nobody, man" he said, rolling over, his eyes still closed.

Back inside the Testarossa, I fell asleep again until another page awakened me. When I called the number to the Southington estate, this time both Don King and John

212

Horne were on the line, screaming and demanding to speak with Mike Tyson.

"Goddammit, Rudy, Mike *will* speak to me!" King kept shouting.

Back inside Brown's apartment, Tyson got on the phone with Don King. It apparently had to do with King insisting that Tyson go somewhere immediately. But MT kept telling King that he didn't want to go, that he wasn't "in the mood," and that he "didn't need to do that." The conversation see-sawed back and forth like that for a few moments. Then, as always, Mike Tyson gave in and agreed to do whatever it was that Don King demanded he do.

"All right, all right! I'll go, I'll go. Just get off my shit, man. Just book us on the next flight." And with that MT hung up and turned to me. "We've got to go to fucking Indianapolis."

"What the fuck?" I couldn't believe it. Here we are in D.C. to spend some time with the family of a Tyson childhood friend who has just been killed, we've driven for hours at race-car speeds to get here, and now King, in the early morning, orders us to hop a plane to Indianapolis on a moment's notice. King had made Tyson cave in by laying a guilt trip on him, that he had to make an appearance for the black children of America and represent his race.

"Look, Rudy," Tyson said. "The motherfucker promised the black children of Indiana that I'll be there at this Black Expo thing. We'll fly in, spend the day, and B Angie B will be there. I'll dip in a little sauce and we be outta' there. It ain't no thing."

Sherry Brown agreed to say her goodbyes at the airport

so she followed us out to Washington National in her Jaguar, a gift from MT. Tyson smooched with Sherry while I headed for the long-term parking garage. When I got back, they were hugging for the last time, and then Brown climbed into the Jaguar and sped away. MT and I walked over to the US Air counter where they were holding two first-class tickets for us on the 11 a.m. flight to Indianapolis. As we approached the gate, I recognized a fat, greasy-looking man waiting to board the same flight. I couldn't believe it! The man was Dale Edwards, one of Don King's nephews.

"Yo, big D, what the fuck you doing here?" I asked him.

"I'm escorting Mike Tyson to Indianapolis," he told us as if we already knew. "DK wanted to make sure I was with him today. We'll meet everybody in Indianapolis."

Something definitely was *very* wrong because it made absolutely no sense that Dale Edwards was in Washington to "escort" Tyson. That had been my job practically every day of my life since May of 1987, and Don King knew I was with Tyson because I had just spoken to King on the phone two hours ago. Dale Edwards *never* had been responsible for bodyguarding Mike Tyson. Edwards wasn't bonded which meant that MT wouldn't have any insurance coverage if there was an incident involving Tyson in any way. At that moment, the flight was called so we all boarded the plane. MT settled in and turned on his Walkman. A moment later, a flight attendant approached me.

"Mr. Gonzalez? The ticket agent needs to speak with you."

"Is there a problem?"

214

"Sir, I really don't know. But you do need to depart the aircraft and see the ticket agent."

I tapped MT's arm, and he removed the earphones. I told him there was a problem with my ticket. "Come on, get off with me." I didn't want to let him out of my sight the way things were going these days.

"No, man, you just take care of it yourself." MT was mourning over the death of a friend and didn't want to be bothered at that time. He put the earphones back on, closed his eyes, and went back to listening to his music.

Cursing under my breath, I walked quickly back through the jetway to the VIP counter where I was informed by a lady that my ticket had been voided.

"Contact Don King Productions," I said impatiently. "There's gotta' be a mistake."

"Sir, you're going to have to do that yourself." She pointed me in the direction of a courtesy phone. I dialed 212-794-2900 and spoke to the receptionist who put me through to Don King who already had returned to New York from Cleveland.

"Yo, Don, what's the problem?" We're here, we're ready to get on the flight. My ticket's been cancelled."

On the speakerphone, with John Horne in the background, King said: "You ain't goin' on that goddamn flight! Now get your ass in the Ferrari and drive it to Ohio, and leave Mike alone."

"Anthony's on the way from LA to meet MT in Indianapolis," Horne added. "So do what the fuck Don tells you to do!"

As I slammed the phone down, Mike Tyson's airplane pulled away from the gate. "Fuck!" I yelled out, grabbed the phone again, and paged Ouie. A couple of minutes passed, and the courtesy phone rang.

"Ouie, something's wrong. MT's alone." I explained the whole series of events which had led us to Washington National Airport. We decided the best thing to do was for me to go to New York which was less than a two-hour drive. Against Don King's orders, I raced the Testarossa toward New York City. A little before 2 p.m., I pulled up in front of the offices of Don King Productions on East 69th Street. I was informed that Don King was nowhere to be found but insisted they keep trying to locate him, Horne, and Holloway. The staff grudgingly made some calls, but apparently these individuals were all *incommunicado.* I paged Horne and Holloway myself but got no response.

My head was throbbing from all the bullshit that had been going on and all the games that were being played. This whole scenario never had happened before. I should have been sitting by Mike Tyson's side on the flight from Washington to Indianapolis on July 18. *I should have been with Mike Tyson every step of the way in Indianapolis, including at his hotel during the early morning hours of July 19, 1991.*

Before I headed west driving the Testarossa back to Southington, Ohio, I stopped by my Mother's apartment in Spanish Harlem and visited with her and some friends for about an hour. Around 9 p.m. that night I was pulling into the grounds of The Big House. At the gatehouse, I asked the security guard to drive me back to the airport so I could catch a flight to D.C. Arriving around midnight, I took a taxi all the way to the service station in Pennsylvania where the highway patrol officer had ordered MT to park the Porsche. After paying cab fare of around $100, I climbed into the Speedster and headed northwest, returning once again to the Southington estate. Because I spent most of the night driving, I parked at service areas for short naps along the way. It was the first drive since I could remember where I respected the speed limits. Around 6 a.m., I again entered the grounds of The Big House.

MT called around seven that morning of July 19, 1991, telling me he would be arriving in Cleveland around 8:40 a.m., and for me to pick him up. Without showering or shaving, I went back out and drove to Cleveland-Hopkins International. Because there was no place to park at the airport, I waited for MT outside the terminal by the curb. Tyson exited the terminal accompanied by Dale Edwards, who then continued on to where he had left his own car in long-term parking. Before I was forced to depart the Indianapolis flight due to my ticket being cancelled, I had left a leather clutch bag in MT's possession. It had contained $10,000 spending money and four condoms, but now I noticed that $4,000 and two of the condoms were missing.

"Who you been fucking with?" I asked him because by this point in time I was concerned with his sexual behavior. Long before he announced it to the world, Magic Johnson had called a meeting with Tyson and Arsenio Hall, two of his closest friends, to tell them that he had been diagnosed as HIV positive. Magic Johnson and MT had shared many of the same groupies. So two things became very important to me after that meeting: keep track of the girls MT had sex with and whether he used a condom.

"I didn't spend no $4,000. No fucking way, man. I don't know what the fuck happened to it."

"What about the two rubbers?"

Tyson told me he had sex with female rapper, B Angie B, and also had used a condom with another girl. On the way back to The Big House, MT told me he was very tired, wanted to crash, and didn't want any noise in the house. I hit the sack until 2 p.m., then went to where the chef was making some lunch. Tyson was snoring away upstairs. I went back to sleep until around 5 p.m. when the chef woke me up, telling me there was a young lady on the phone who wanted to speak with Mr. Tyson. I informed the chef that MT was not to be disturbed under any circumstances. The chef already knew that, but the young lady had insisted that she be put through to Mr. Tyson.

"I'll take the call in my room, " I told her. A moment later I punched the flashing hold button.

"I want to talk to Mike Tyson."

"He's not available."

"Who's this?"

"This is his personal aide. What can I do for you?"

"I need to talk to Mike."

"What's your name?"

"This is Desiree Washington." I thought at first it was "Desree," a Tyson girlfriend, who lived in D.C. When I asked her about the weather there, I then realized I had made a mistake.

"You must have me confused with somebody else," she said, her voice much colder now. "This is the Desiree Washington. He met me yesterday."

"He's sleeping now. Leave me a message, and I'll make sure he gets back to you.."

"I'll call him back," she said and hung up.

I went back to sleep until around 8 p.m. Later, I was in the kitchen when the phone rang. MT was still upstairs resting.

"Mr. Tyson's residence. May I help you?"

On the other end I recognized the same voice I had heard earlier in the day. "I want to speak with Mike Tyson."

By her tone, I could tell she had developed an attitude. "This is Rudy again. Mr. Tyson is still not available."

"I need to speak with him now," she said.

He doesn't want to be disturbed right now."

"When is he going to call me back?" It was clear that this young lady was getting very annoyed at being put off.

"I don't know, miss. He has many priority messages to return."

I now was sure MT must have just met her. She didn't yet understand the rules of the celebrity game. Famous people are very busy people who attend to a lot of very important matters when they're not performing for the public. And unless you were known to be a very important person, then you took a place in line like everybody else.

"If you'll just be patient, I'm sure he'll get back to you."

"Listen," she snapped at me. "Mike Tyson better talk

to me now. It's better sooner than later." Then she hung up.

That was the second and only other time I ever spoke to Desiree Washington. Later I would think how ironic it was that Don King had ordered Mike Tyson to run an errand from *Washington* where he ended up meeting *Washington.*

Not long after I got off the phone with Desiree Washington, Tyson came downstairs looking for food. In the meantime, I had spoken to Anthony in LA to catch up on things. Anthony hadn't gone to Indianapolis because John Horne told him there was no need to travel half-way across the country and interrupt his honeymoon when I was going to be with MT *anyway*. When Tyson entered the kitchen, I told him that me and Anthony were very pissed that we had been lied to.

"We'll deal with that shit later. Let me eat, man."

"A bitch, Desiree Washington, has been calling you. What's up with her? She seems to have a problem."

His eyes widened. "I don't wanna' talk to her. She was playing games with me in the hotel." Tyson said that after they did "the wild thing" she "freaked out."

Apparently, the young lady had been upset because MT didn't escort her downstairs to the limousine waiting to take her back to her own hotel room. Tyson never escorted anybody down from an apartment or hotel room after sex. That always had been a job left to his bodyguards.

"Why did you let Don King take me off the plane? Me or Anthony should've been with you."

Tyson just shrugged. "Listen, we're going to bury Demencio in Brooklyn. Pull out a black suit and get ready to fly to New York."

That same evening of July 19, 1991, we got two crank calls at The Big House. I had answered "Tyson residence," and could tell someone was on the other end, checking out who answered, before hanging up. We left very early on July 20 to catch our flight to New York to attend Demencio's funeral. After the burial the next day, Tyson went out to dinner with a group of friends from the old days. He was trying his best to cheer everybody up. He wanted them to remember Demencio as somebody who over the years had made them laugh.

Don King had been trying to get in touch with Tyson the entire morning, but MT didn't want to talk to him. Apparently, King wanted to speak with Tyson about MT going directly to Caesar's Palace to schedule a fight with Holyfield. We were driving around with Anthony and Sherry Brown, when Tyson told me to take them to Don King's townhouse. MT wanted to discuss what was going on with the Holyfield fight. We were greeted by the maid, and Tyson asked her to see about getting some buffalo wings. The maid showed us to the living room and turned on the television. We were just hanging out telling jokes when a news bulletin came on.

"On July 19, former heavyweight champion, Mike Tyson, is alleged to have raped a beauty contestant, Desiree Washington, at the Black Expo in Indianapolis."

All of us were in shock, except Mike Tyson. Instead, he looked very disappointed, like someone whom he had trusted had let him down. Desiree Washington never ran to a hospital or the police after that early-morning encounter with Tyson in Room 606 at the Canterbury Hotel. In fact, she had called The Big House twice during the afternoon of that same day wanting to speak with MT. I was the one who had answered the phone and taken her messages on those two occasions. *Tyson never called her back that day.* Desiree Washington waited until the next day before she reported to authorities that she had been raped by Mike Tyson.

After a few moments, Tyson said in a low voice. "I can't understand why they're doin' this to me."

There was a long silence as we just sat there not knowing what to say. A few moments later, Don King strolled into the living room. He had just entered the house and was still wearing a leather jacket which he took off and threw on a table.

"Now you need my help, nigger!" he boomed in Tyson's direction. "Your dick got you in trouble now! Goddammit, Mike, now you need me!"

MT didn't say anything. He just lowered his head as if he were a small child being scolded.

Don King took over even more of Mike Tyson's affairs. He now became entrusted with the job of his legal defense. An indictment was handed down by a Marion County grand jury on September 9, 1991: one count of rape, two counts of deviate sexual conduct, and one count of confinement. Tyson pleaded "not guilty," because, he maintained, the sexual encounter between him and Desiree Washington in the early morning hours of July 19 was consensual. Don King retained Vince Fuller, a sixty-year-old lawyer from the D.C. firm of Williams and Connolly, who apparently already had represented King in another matter. Now, Fuller was given the task of preparing Tyson's defense in the rape trial scheduled for January 27, 1992 in Indianapolis.

In October of 1991, we were in New York City staying at Tyson's new condo near the United Nations, a smaller apartment than the one in the Marlborough House. We were going to go out that night, but the Lamborghini jeep parked in the garage was disabled with a flat tire. We couldn't change it at the time because you needed four guys to work with the 180 lb. tires. I mentioned to MT that there was a Mercedes parked in Celia Tuckman's building on 39th Street and Second Avenue. Tuckman's apartment was one of the three which we discovered MT was paying for, even though she was a vice-president of Don King Productions and also one of King's mistresses. On two separate occasions I walked in on them having sex. She would sit on top of his lap jumping up and down. I once told MT that I had caught them. Tyson made sure he mentioned it to Don King, that we knew he was screwing Celia Tuckman. King replied: "Gotta' fuck them Jews anyway you can."

The Mercedes 500SEL was a "corporate car" of the Mike Tyson Fan Club which was wholly-owned by the King family. Tyson ordered me to go pick it up so I grabbed a taxi to the Churchill Towers. The car was gorgeous, a $100,000 white 500SEL with a blue interior, spoiler kit, and 16" wheels. The first thing I noticed inside the vehicle was the name "Don King" engraved on the seats. That night Tyson was out with some buddies and drank champagne. At one point while we were driving around Tyson got pissed, turned to me, and said: "Fuck this shit up." I was confused and didn't understand what he meant. MT explained that he wanted me to systematically start smashing up this vehicle, a demolition derby with any objects I could find. At around 3 a.m. on Lexington Avenue, I began slamming the Mercedes into parking meters. I'll never forget the look we got from the parking attendant back at the Chuchill Towers. We heard the next day that Don King and Celia Tuckman went ballistic when they saw what was left of the Mercedes parked in Celia Tuckman's spot.

In the meantime, Tyson returned to Las Vegas to train for a fight with Holyfield at Caesar's Palace scheduled for November 8, 1991. About a month before the bout, Tyson got injured under very suspicious circumstances. John Horne appeared at the gym with some gravity boots. He told Richard Giachetti to "back up, I'm training Mike this afternoon." Horne told Giachetti that they needed to work on MT's abdominals because Holyfield was a "stomach puncher." For a long time, Giachetti had been trying to use his own proven methods to get Tyson into top fighting form. However, there always seemed to be interference with his program. So by this time, a very frustrated Giachetti simply said to Horne: "What the fuck you know about training? You ain't no trainer," and walked out.

John Horne knew less about boxing than I did about building a nuclear bomb. Horne, Aaron Snowell, and Carl King, who also were present at the training session, helped slip the boots onto Tyson's feet, and then hung him upside down on a bar. MT had never used this training method before. Tyson started to do his situps and, after doing about 100, on an upward swing, we heard a pop. Tyson had torn a cartilage in his rib cage, an injury not serious enough to prevent him from fighting anybody on the planet, including Evander Holyfield, a month later. Even if Mike Tyson had three broken ribs and a hangover, he could knock "Real Deal" Holyfield on his ass within a few seconds. However, this minor injury was a godsend for Don King who immediately announced to the world that his fighter was out of commission, necessitating the cancelling of the match with Holyfield. When Tyson heard this, he was enraged. But there also was the rape trial in Indianapolis which was just around the corner to contend with, and Don King was running that show. The time was not ripe for an ugly confrontation with the man strategizing your legal defense. *The Miami Herald* reported that the Tyson-Holyfield fight was expected to be "the first

$100 million bout and its postponement may still set a new mark—the most expensive party never thrown....The trial means that the party might never happen."

We returned to The Big House in Southington, Ohio. Soon, Mike Tyson's life took a final nosedive into the toilet while Don King kept telling him there was no way he was going to be convicted in Indianapolis. Tyson started hanging out with a guy named Iceberg Slim, a pimp with some very bad habits, whom Don King and John Horne had introduced to Tyson. There also were a lot of other low-life characters who started hanging around The Big House during this period. They would encourage Tyson to act like an idiot and be offensive, trying to deter his thoughts from the serious business at hand, preparing for the rape trial in Indianapolis. There also was a new "rap" being laid on him by King, Iceberg Slim, and others surrounding him, that Tyson's legal problems in Indianapolis were the "white man's fault." I could see how Tyson was turning increasingly angrier at everybody and everything in the world.

It was also during the period of mid-1991 that luxury automobiles in MT's inventory, now numbering around one hundred, had to have their registrations renewed. It turned out that they were being re-registered in the name of The Mike Tyson Fan Club in Orwell, Ohio, a corporation wholly-owned and operated by Don King Productions. Debbie King, Don King's daughter, was Vice-President of this organization. The $52,000 check made out to her name, which we discovered that watershed day on June 12, 1991 in MT's Las Vegas bedroom, was her salary check. Now, back in Ohio after the incident in Indianapolis, I remembered that Henrietta King, Don King's wife, had signed Mike Tyson's name on the renewal forms for these cars. Again, my Panasonic copier-scanner came in very handy to document what was going on.

The last time I was with Mike Tyson was in late January of 1992 at the Capitol Hilton at 16th Street, N.W. in Washington, D.C. That's where he was staying while meeting with Vince Fuller a few days prior to the trial scheduled in Indianapolis for January 27, 1992. It was only the second time they had met since the allegations of rape against Tyson more than six months ago. The first meeting had been right after Tyson voluntarily surrendered subsequent to the handing down of the indictment in Marion County. That first meeting at Williams & Connolly in September had lasted barely ten minutes. Present also were Don King, Anthony Pitts, John Horne and myself. Vince Fuller only seemed to be concerned with what Mike Tyson was going to wear the day of trial. So I decided to speak up and tell Fuller about the two calls from Desiree Washington to The Big House on July 20. An expression of shock crossed Vince Fuller's face.

Don King jumped up out of his chair. "That's bullshit! Don't believe him!"

"He's right, Don," Tyson said.

"Goddammit, Rudy, don't ever say that shit again! It ain't got nothing to do with this so just keep your mother-fucking mouth shut!"

Anthony turned to Tyson. "Why don't we just say we

228

were with you, MT?"

John Horne started yelling. "Shut the fuck up! Stop bullshitting."

Then Don King began telling Tyson about the William Kennedy Smith case and how he didn't have to worry about losing. "You'll get off. Don't listen to those crazy motherfuckers."

During this entire exchange, Vince Fuller never said a word. When we left, Don King and John Horne had convinced Tyson that, in the worst case scenario, he only would get a slap on the wrist. We returned to the Southington estate where Tyson's social behavior continued to spiral downward under the watchful eyes of Don King associates, like Iceberg Slim, and family members who systematically were dragging my boss through the gutter. As the trial date rapidly approached, I was considering bringing in a team of legal experts to work with Tyson and start preparing for trial because there was no preparation going on between Tyson and Vince Fuller. We had flown to D.C. several times between September of 1991 and January of 1992. *However, the only ones to meet with Vince Fuller were John Horne and Don King.* John Horne instructed me and Anthony "not to bother MT anymore" about the case because there would be no problem. MT and I usually just hung outside the law firm's building talking to girls while the others met inside.

The only other trip where Tyson actually met with Vince Fuller to prepare the case was a few days before trial. MT had flown to Washington with Don King. I drove the Lincoln-Continental limousine with passengers Anthony Pitts,

Isadore Bolton, and a relation of Don King named Craig whose main role was to procure women and organize group sex. Craig also was responsible for taking videos while he and others hanging around him encouraged MT to act stupid and obnoxious on camera. The night before he flew to D.C., with the possibility that he might lose the case now finally sinking in, MT gave me final instructions. I packed the limo with several trunks of his clothing, approximately $1.3 million in cash, and what certainly was several million more in diamond and gold jewelry.

"Collect everything," MT had told me as we emptied his safe in The Big House. "I want you to take care of my business. I don't want any of those niggers in my house. Don't let anybody fuck with my shit." He was referring to Don King, John Horne, Rory Holloway, and their intimates who had been leeching themselves for so long onto the Tyson money machine.

"Rudy, I've never taken care of you," he said as he finished gathering up the last of his things. "You've got one big one coming." By that Tyson meant he was going to give me a million dollars.

When I didn't respond, he turned around and found me standing at attention, like I had thousands of times before for more than five years. Even when his world might soon be coming to an end, even when he was most vulnerable, even when he was entrusting me and nobody else with the most important details of his life, I still was acting as respectfully and professionally as I had when I became his servant for the first time on a cold winter night back in November of 1986.

"Rudy, if anything happens to me, just take

care of your shit."

Looking at his face for what would be the last time, it seemed to me that Mike Tyson had convinced himself during these last moments in his master bedroom at The Big House in Southington, Ohio, that forces around him were going to take him out of the picture regardless of the truth.

"The Final Round"

On a cold but skyblue-clear day, January 25, 1992, I pulled the Lincoln-Continental limousine up to the entrance of The Capitol Hilton on 16th Street, N.W. in Washington, D.C. This was where Mike Tyson was staying for his second meeting with Vince Fuller, just days before trial would start in Indianapolis. John Horne was waiting, ready to pounce on us the moment we arrived.

"Come over here," Horne ordered all of us, cocking his head in the direction of the lobby.

I grabbed the Louis Vuitton vanity case which contained millions in jewelry owned by Mike Tyson and went inside followed by Anthony.

"Anthony, MT wants you to go back to California until this is all over," Horne began. "Then you're back on the team. Isadore, you go up and start unpacking everything. And now," Horne said, turning to me with his weasel smile and an outstretched hand. "It's your turn. Hand over the safe box with all the jewelry."

When I refused, Horne began yelling "Hand over the box, hand over the box!"

Don King appeared at Horne's side. "Goddammit, take the fucking jewelry from him. I'm tired of this shit!"

There was no way I was going to deliver millions of MT's valuables to these two jerks. I demanded to see Tyson, but King and Horne refused and continued to verbally threaten me, their body language sending a message that they might pounce on me any second. I decided to pull out the company's 9mm Glock semi-automatic pistol to prevent this, keeping it at my side rather than pointing it in their direction. At that moment, secret service agents appeared out of nowhere and bolted toward me. Apparently, they were there to protect political figures and be on the lookout for behavior which might constitute a danger to them. After the initial yelling and screaming, I was able to produce credentials, proving that I worked for Mike Tyson Productions. The D.C. police were called in and interrogation began to try and sort things out. I informed the cops that there were millions of dollars of Mike Tyson's personal property in my custody and care which was not going to be released to anyone except Mike Tyson. Don King denied he had tried to take possession and quickly disappeared from the hotel lobby. John Horne told the police that he worked for Mike Tyson, and there would be no problem as long as I agreed to release the property to him.

Because I had credentials and was wearing a Team Tyson jacket, the cops believed that I had certain authority over this property. However, they needed instructions directly from Mike Tyson how to resolve this dispute and sent someone to meet with him. A few minutes later, Rory Holloway came down to the lobby bearing a settlement proposal. The valuables would be placed in the hotel safe. At the same time, my gun was confiscated. Two officers had counseled me to do so voluntarily. With Tyson under indictment, and perhaps a convicted felon within days, Mike Tyson Productions probably wouldn't be bondable any longer. Therefore, any problems arising over my carrying this weapon might cause Mike Tyson Productions some legal

233

troubles. To this day for all I know, the company's 9mm Glock semi-automatic still is collecting dust in the property room of a D.C. police station.

John Horne confronted me one more time as I was about to leave the Capitol Hilton. "Give me the fucking computer, Rudy."

"Fuck you, I ain't giving you shit!"

"Give me the fucking computer you're always writing in."

Everybody knew about the Sharp "Wizard," a wallet-sized device which I always carried with me, and on which I always seemed to be tapping away, entering or recalling information. I had been using it to log, not just phone numbers and scheduling matters, but also things which were important to what was happening in Mike Tyson's life, such as his sexual encounters and whether he used a condom. The Wizard was used to keep track of all of MT's jewelry that he gave to his numerous one-night stands. Also recorded were the confrontations with Don King. Horne needed the Wizard to get his hands on certain information and report back to Don King, such as the location of jewelry and automobiles.

"I ain't giving you my fucking computer."

"Give me the fucking computer!" Horne again demanded.

I turned around and saw the local police still lingering around the lobby. I figured that this issue was going to be resolved the same way as the Tyson personal property. So I pulled the computer from my shirt pocket, pressed the reset button wiping out the master memory, and ejected the disc, slipping it into my shirt pocket. I turned back to Horne and handed him a computer with no information. He never had a clue.

Boarding a Trump Shuttle flight to LaGuardia, I returned to my Mother's apartment in the housing project in Spanish Harlem where I stayed for awhile, following the progress of MT's trial which began on January 27. On February 10, when the verdict of guilty on all counts was announced, I put my head down and cried. It was the end of my world.

Two days after Mike Tyson's trial was over, I took some of my savings and headed back to Brazil. It seemed like I had to travel thousands of miles to another country before my head would be able to clear. As I went over everything that had happened, it became apparent to me that there were too many forces working against Mike Tyson to give him a fair chance. In the aftermath of the trial, a number of people were talking, and articles were being written, criticizing the handling of Tyson's defense. Well-known boxing figure, Ferdie Pacheco, wrote in *Boxing Illustrated* that "huge errors" had been made by Fuller and his team, who reportedly received $2 million for their handling of the case. "By conceding that Mike Tyson was a ghetto animal" in his opening statement, Fuller was sending the wrong message to the jury, `Well, maybe he didn't rape this girl, but he sure raped a lot of others.'" Pacheco concluded that "Mike Tyson had no chance of a fair trial."

Robert Simels, a lawyer who counts many athletes among his clients, was quoted in the February 24, 1992 issue of *Time* magazine that Fuller "was probably not the right choice to bring into Indianapolis. They certainly needed a strong local female counsel. A woman could have handled parts of the examination—the questions about panty shields—which are much more sensitive for a male attorney to be hitting a proposed rape victim with." Simels also described other "defense blunders," such as permitting Tyson to testify to the grand jury, then "allowing Mike to come up with a different story during the trial." This made Tyson look like a liar, and a very bad one at that, "fulfilling any juror's suspicions about the boxer's brutality." The *Time* article made several observations, including that women didn't come to Tyson to "tame the beast" but rather "to unleash him." "It's possible that at 2 a.m. on July 19 in Room 606 at the Canterbury Hotel, Tyson was as astonished by Washington's reaction as she was by his actions. Tyson runs with the wrong crowd. Many of his friends are paid help, hired as extra muscle or procurers. Don King, the convicted killer who promotes Tyson's bouts, is a sneaky-smooth fighter in smoke-filled rooms."

Sonja Steptoe, a well-known journalist, writing in an article entitled "A Damnable Defense," recounted some of Fuller's inexplicable strategies. According to Steptoe, Fuller had told the jury that when Tyson came to Indianapolis, after having just won a bout with Razor Ruddock, that he was anxious to "relax for the first time in weeks." I knew that statement wasn't true. Tyson hadn't been "anxious to relax" at the Black Expo. Instead, Tyson had wanted to stay with Demencio's mother in

236

D.C. when we got that fateful call from Don King demanding that MT go to Indianapolis.

Later, I obtained a copy of Vince Fuller's complete opening statement. In it he stated to the jury: "I want...you to understand how Mr. Tyson happens to be here in Indianapolis. He had been invited for several years to come to Black Expo by the Reverend Williams...He didn't come. This year, by coincidence, in the Black Expo program was a young woman singer by the name of B Angie B...Mr. Tyson has kept track of her engagement schedule in the hopes that he'll be able to follow along with her and visit with her as she moves through the country...So now he's relaxing for the first time in weeks...He arranges with B Angie B to meet her in Indianapolis and arranges further for the both of them to go to Cleveland, Ohio, on the morning of the 19th of July because she is performing in Cleveland, Ohio on the evening of the 19th of July. When he knows he's coming to Indianapolis, he does call the Reverend Williams...to tell him he will be here and would be happy to do what little he can for the Black Expo.." About the morning of July 19, Fuller said: "Meanwhile, Mr. Tyson is at his hotel. He's awakened at 4:30 in the morning, dresses, proceeds to the airport where he meets B Angie B and they fly to Cleveland in a somewhat jovial mood." These statements of fact were bullshit. And Tyson wasn't in a jovial mood accompanied by B Angie B when he came out of the terminal at the Cleveland airport. Instead, he walked out with Dale Edwards, the wannabe "bodyguard" who had been in the lobby of the Canterbury Hotel, instead of in MT's hotel room, when the "incident" occurred.

Sonja Steptoe also wrote that "during the trial Fuller went to great lengths to elicit testimony" about Tyson's "sex-crazed" conduct toward the beauty-pageant contestants. In effect, Fuller was saying to the jury: Tyson is your worst nightmare—a vulgar, socially inept, sex-obsessed black athlete." Steptoe observed that the defense team had attempted to introduce expert testimony about the size of Tyson's penis to explain the vaginal abrasions, which tactic later was spoofed on *Saturday Night Live*. She concluded by saying that Tyson was portrayed by his own lawyer as "a stereotypical savage black man run amok." Fuller also stated to the jury that: "At the opening ceremony...Interestingly enough, Jesse Jackson was there, and Jesse Jackson beckons to Mr. Tyson to come over to him at a time he's been talking to Miss Washington. Mr. Tyson utters a vulgarity and indicates: `I don't want to go spend time with Jesse Jackson. He just wants to preach at me. I don't really want to do that.'" Is this the way for Tyson's lawyer to "enhance" his client's image in his opening statement, or is this instead something the *prosecutor* should be highlighting?

I came across other articles where events at trial were reported. "Even Mr. Tyson seemed a little put off by Mr. Fuller at first," *The National Law Journal* stated. "He began the trial sitting next to him, but later moved between [two other] defense lawyers." Fuller's questioning of Desiree Washington was characterized as "artless, plodding, and remarkably lacking in style," by Dan Carpenter of the

Indianapolis Star. I learned that Camille Ewald was present at the trial and held her "son's" hand during part of the proceedings.

Desiree Washington told the jury that Tyson had met her on July 18 during a rehearsal for the Miss Black America pageant which was being held in Indianapolis. Tyson had been *taken* there by the Reverend Williams, a Don King intimate. Why was Tyson taken there where he was videotaped being "disrespectful and offensive" to the contestants? This videotape later was played to the jury. Wasn't Tyson instead supposed to be at the Black Expo fulfilling Don King's "commitment to the black children?" At the rehearsal, Tyson was *directed* to hug one of the women, and he embraced Washington, who was positioned close to him. Washington agreed to go out with Tyson that night and gave him her hotel room number.

One contestant testified that Washington said to her when Tyson walked into the rehearsal: "That's $20 million." There also was testimony that Washington had posed for a picture in Tyson's lap, sat there longer than the other girls, and had to be *pried off.* Contestant Madeline Whittington saw Washington in the ladies room after she met Tyson and had agreed to go out with him. "Of course I'm going. This is Mike Tyson. He's got a lot of money. He's dumb. You see what Robin Givens got out of him." Contestant Cecilia Alexander overheard this conversation. Tanya St. Claire, also attending the pageant, related other comments made by Desiree Washington, including speculation about the size of Tyson's penis. Washington talked about wanting a rich man, a man with money. "Robin Givens had him. I can have him too...He's dumb anyway." Washington's comments about Tyson being "dumb" were also heard by Contestant Caroline Jones. It was very sad to read these things said by Desiree Washington about a very good man, a man with whom I had been almost every day for nearly five years, a man who already had suffered enormous deceit and betrayal before July 19, 1991.

If Tyson's behavior had been so outrageous at the rehearsal, why would a "nice girl" agree to his "request?" Tyson phoned Washington at 1:36 a.m., and she soon was picked up at the Omni Severin Hotel in a limousine provided by the Black Expo. Tyson's "chauffeur," some lady named Virginia Foster, testified that Tyson had "begged" Washington to join him while he made a brief stop back at his room in the Canterbury Hotel.

"And he said something about a bodyguard," Washington testified. Mike Tyson's "bodyguard" that night was Dale Edwards, Don King's nephew who without warning mysteriously had appeared at the US Air gate for our flight to Indianapolis, the flight I was kicked off because Don King Productions cancelled my ticket. I had been told that it didn't matter because Anthony Pitts was coming from LA to be with Tyson *anyway.* And Anthony had been told that he didn't have to go to Indianapolis because I was going to be with MT *anyway.* Did Mike Tyson believe that Dale Edwards was going to do what a bodyguard was supposed to do, protect the celebrity from false accusations by being *near him at all times?* It later came out that Dale Edwards remained in the lobby while Tyson and Washington went to Room 606 where the alleged incident took place. Dale Edwards testified before the grand jury. However, Edwards was not called by the defense and, in fact, was *nowhere to be found* around the courthouse during the trial.

In his hotel, according to Washington, Tyson asked about her home and school, and then started talking about his pigeons. "And I thought that was great," Washington testified, "because I love animals." Tyson had told me that part of the "weird thing" about Washington was that she seemed to know a lot about his personal life *before* they met, including the fact that he loved pigeons. The prosecutor specially-appointed to handle this case, Gregory Garrison, said in his opening statement that Tyson had thrown Washington onto the bed "like a rag doll," while his "massive forearm" held her down. Washington testified that the bedspread had been pulled back. "I glanced over and saw the defendant in his underwear...on the bed. He was just sitting there....I was terrified." Something was *very* wrong here as well. In the more than five years I had known him, Mike Tyson *never* had sex or slept in a bed. If he had sexually assaulted somebody, it would never have been on a bed.

I later obtained a copy of the brief filed by Alan Dershowitz and his team of lawyers who handled MT's appeal. In it I learned that one witness, Claudia Jordan, testified that Washington told her "that the incident occurred on the floor." If I had been interviewed by Vince Fuller and permitted to testify at trial, I could have corroborated Claudia Jordan's

241

testimony about Tyson's habit of having sex on the floor, never the bed. This would tend to show that Washington was prone to fabricate a story at trial. And about the "underwear issue," Mike Tyson had traveled to Indianapolis on July 18, 1991 without wearing underwear and did not have a change of clothing because we hadn't been scheduled to take any trips. Tyson never wore regular underwear anyway due to his massive thigh muscles. Tyson travelled to Indianapolis on July 18 in a Versace summer suit with a "jock strap" built into the pants. The suit was designed for the wearer not to use underwear which would have been exposed through the sheer silk garment and looked tacky. I could have testified to all of these facts if Tyson's attorneys had cared to find out about them and use them in his defense at the trial.

Another interesting section is contained in the appellate brief. Apparently, three women, Carla J. Martin, Pamela Lawrence, and Renee Neal, observed that Tyson and Washington were embracing and kissing *in the limousine* as they arrived at the Canterbury Hotel. "They were all over each other," according to Martin. Neal saw them holding hands as they entered the lobby of the hotel. These witnesses would have *directly contradicted* Washington's testimony that she followed *behind* Tyson in the lobby and did *not* hold hands with him. Rather, Washington testified that she was *surprised* by Tyson's advances on her *once inside* Room 606. These witnesses were never permitted to testify at trial. The defense team never found them before trial. Rather, the witnesses contacted the Black Expo themselves after trial already had begun.

The trial judge refused to let Martin, Lawrence, and Neal testify due to late notification. With a $2 million budget, why didn't the defense "team" locate these individuals during the six months it had to prepare for trial? After all, these three witnesses were present at the Canterbury at that time because they had gone to retrieve a bag Martin had left there. This was something an amateur private investigator should have discovered. Had these witnesses been allowed to testify about Washington's conduct *prior* to going up with Tyson to Room 606, a different outcome might have occurred at trial. In fact, on March 25, 1995, the Associated Press reported that David Vahle, a member of the Tyson jury, and four fellow members "have developed doubts about the former boxing champion's guilt." These doubts result in part from their learning about the existence of "the three defense witnesses who were not permitted to testify at the trial."

There also was the issue of the use of a condom. Desiree Washington claimed that she asked Tyson to put one on, but that he didn't have one. I knew that he did, and Tyson had told me he used one with "another girl" besides B Angie B. This also was another contradiction which would have tended to show that Washington was capable of inventing certain critical facts. If you use a rubber, chances are you're not conducting yourself like a rapist.

And, of course, I could have testified about the *two calls* Desiree Washington made to the Tyson residence during the afternoon of July 19. And how Washington was offended because Tyson hadn't been available to speak with her. This was the day *before* she reported being sexually assaulted by Mike Tyson. Vince Fuller already knew about this fact five months before Mike Tyson went to trial accused of being a rapist at that first meeting in his offices in D.C. Virginia Foster, the "chauffeur," testified that when Washington entered the limousine after leaving Tyson's room, the first thing she said was: "I can't believe him. I can't believe him. Who does he think he is?" Desiree Washington didn't sound like a woman attacked. She did sound like a woman scorned. My testimony, if Vince Fuller had cared at all about this critical information, would have shown Desiree Washington's *state of mind* a day before she reported her encounter with Tyson as a rape.

If I had been allowed to do my job, instead of being kicked off the flight to Indianapolis and held back in D.C., then I would have been in Room 606 of the Canterbury Hotel while Tyson had sex with Desiree Washington. I also would have escorted Washington, not only downstairs to the waiting limousine, but also back to her own hotel room. For many years, a fundamental part of my duties for MT was to make women feel special after having sex with Tyson. MT got an "F" in bedside manner, but he *wasn't a rapist*. And I could have corroborated that if Vince Fuller and his high-priced Washington defense "team" had cared at all to have my testimony. However, a very different type of preparation, which did not even include my input, had been laid out for the defense of Mike Tyson.

244

One survey taken by an Indianapolis tv station revealed that 60% disagreed with the guilty verdict. On April 9, 1994, *The Miami Herald* reported that "an Indiana Court of Appeals ruled that a judge must review claims that a woman Mike Tyson was convicted of raping had earlier falsely accused a high school classmate of rape. Affidavits were obtained from Wayne Walker, his mother, and one of his football teammates that said Desiree Washington in 1989 falsely accused Walker, a classmate at Coventry High School in Rhode Island, of rape."

Before the rape trial, Desiree Washington told the world that she didn't bring charges against Tyson "to take his career away." She did it because he "needed help." There had been reports that Washington was offered up to $750,000 but refused to take any money. However, once Tyson was convicted, thereby establishing his liability toward her as a matter of law, she filed a civil suit for an unspecified amount of damages. The case has been working its way steadily through the Indiana courts. There are sections of the Dershowitz appellate brief which are "sealed," meaning the public does not have access to them. I have learned that at least some of these sections relate to Desiree Washington's civil suit.

After many months had passed, there came a time when I would be asked to get back into the business of working for a professional fighter. Gladys Rosa, a Don King employee who handled Hispanic boxers, asked for my assistance to set up a fight for my old childhood friend, Hector "Macho" Camacho. I remember that she used to shiver at the prospect of being left alone with Don King and would beg me to stay with her at certain times. Gladys Rosa told me that she wanted my assistance to arrange a fight between Camacho and Julio Cesar Chavez, a Mexican fighter who was being handled by Don King Productions. I didn't know at that time Camacho's contract with the Duvas was coming up for renewal. I told Gladys Rosa I would think about it and get back to her. Camacho was staying with his mother in the same roach-infested housing project, Jefferson Houses, on East 115th Street, where my Mother was living. Two months had gone by when Hector Camacho finally decided that he wanted to have the meeting requested by Gladys Rosa. Camacho's corporation, HC, Inc., hired me at $1,000 per day to accompany Macho and Gladys Rosa to South Florida to finalize arrangements for the Julio Cesar Chavez match. We boarded a plane for the West Palm Beach airport. Our destination was Don King's estate in an exclusive community called Foxe Chase located in Delray Beach. It was purchased, as I understand it, for around $1 million about the time Mike Tyson went on trial for rape in Indianapolis. Don King Productions had relocated its operations to Ft. Lauderdale, Florida.

That day Camacho was "jonesing," meaning he needed to do some coke really bad. Unfortunately, my friend had been having problems with cocaine since his early teens. He believed in *santeria,* the spirit-religion practiced by some Hispanics, originating in Africa and brought to the new world by the slaves. Camacho believed that he was protected by a certain spirit named "Titan" who shared his own spirit. Titan took him to the dark side but also cared for him and saved him from harm. To satisfy Titan, Camacho would "feed" him by ingesting cocaine. During the flight I learned that Gladys Rosa had promised Camacho some coke, and it was easy to see that he was desperate to get some.

Don King's driver, Isadore Bolton, picked us up at the airport, and soon we were pulling up to an enormous round residence, all done in white marble, which sits on a lake. In the distance, there was a pier with a speedboat tied up to it. Bolton ushered us inside where we were greeted by two huge stone lions on pedestals guarding the foyer. I could see the look of amazement on Camacho's face. He wasn't used to this kind of wealth whereas I had been around it just about every day for the past six years. Mike Tyson made more in one fight than Camacho had made in his entire career. Bolton went to another room where Don King was sitting with a couple of guys and announced our arrival. We sat around waiting on leather couches in the room behind the stone lions. King strolled in, greeted Camacho, glanced over at me without acknowledging my presence, and then turned to Gladys Rosa.

"Are the contracts signed?"

"No, he didn't sign yet."

At that moment, Camacho jumped up. "I ain't signing nothing until I get some blow!"

King motioned to Rosa to follow him into his private office. About five minutes later, Rosa returned carrying a leather portfolio engraved with the Don King Productions logo. She sat with Camacho on the end of the sofa and opened up the portfolio, extracting a manila folder which contained the fight contract. She also produced a sandwich baggie which contained a white, powdery substance.

In Spanish, Rosa said: "I've got ten grams, but the contract must be signed now. And there will be more after it's signed." She added that Camacho would be receiving $100,000 for fighting Chavez, and that he was going to train in Cleveland at "Mike Tyson's camp."

At that moment I realized I had become an unwitting participant in a trap. This trip wasn't about Gladys Rosa promoting for her own account a fight against King-owned Julio Cesar Chavez. I had been operating under the impression that I was going to help train Camacho, along with Gladys Rosa, for the Chavez fight. Suddenly, I learned that this whole charade was about delivering Camacho to Don King so that he would sign on as exclusive property of Don King Productions, rather than renew his contract with the Duvas. Now there was no further need for either me or Gladys Rosa. Hector "Macho" Camacho agreed that day to all terms and conditions proposed to him, switching him over to Don King Productions and away from the Duvas, just to get some blow in his nose as soon as possible.

"Don't forget about my hundred g's," Camacho said as we started to leave. "And the rest of my *perico.*" The Spanish word *"perico"* means parakeet. It also is slang for cocaine because you might start talking like one if you do some blow. Hector Camacho went off to Cleveland to train with Don King Productions. I returned to Spanish Harlem once again out of a job.

This wasn't the only fighter with whom Gladys Rosa used this strategy to get results for Don King. She also betrayed Julio Cesar Chavez by making him believe that she was an "independent Latin boxing consultant," serving as his business-relations manager and interpreter. In fact, Rosa had been a long-time Don King Productions employee, "negoti- ating deals" so that King would have the upper hand. She didn't hesitate to use cocaine to entice Chavez into the King stable and manipulate him. Unfortunately, Julio Cesar Chavez developed a very bad drug habit. He sought help in Mexico by committing himself to a rehab facility. But on the day of his release, Gladys Rosa was waiting at the door with fight contracts and more cocaine.

In the fall of 1993, I went to Las Vegas to look up an old girlfriend who was working in guest relations at The Golden Nugget. What I originally had planned to be a brief encounter with Heather turned into a six-month stay with her. During that time, she let me use her house, car, beeper, and employee meal tickets good at all the hotels. One night I was having dinner alone at the Showboat when an elderly, very polite black gentleman approached me. He had been sitting at a nearby table with his wife and older children. I could tell by the way he looked that he had lived a very hard life. The old man mentioned that he had worked in VIP housekeeping at the Hilton where Don King had maintained a penthouse suite even though his regular residence had been set up at The Mirage. It had been the man's job to take care of that particular area of the Hilton. This same suite was where King and John Horne used to meet alone for hours on end. I remember thinking it was weird that King and Horne would be together in closed quarters for such long periods of time. The black gentleman had remembered me from the days when I was constantly at Mike Tyson's side while he was preparing for the two Razor Ruddock fights.

The old man told me that he was concerned about what had happened to Mike Tyson and found it strange that he was found guilty and put in prison. Then the man related a very bizarre story. Sometime in the spring of 1991, during the period of the two Tyson-Ruddock fights, he was cleaning the King penthouse suite in the Hilton when he noticed a large number of files in the master bedroom. Thinking they contained fight photos, he sat on the bed and started looking through them.   Instead of finding what he expected, he noticed that these files contained information and crime scene photos relating to rape cases.   To him it seemed like somebody had been "studying up" on something pretty important. He remembered in particular that one of the cases dealt with somebody named Alexander Pantages.   Later, I would learn that Pantages was the owner of a chain of theaters who in 1929 was convicted of rape and sentenced to fifty years. After a successful appeal, Pantages won a new trial in 1931 in which he was found not guilty. On her deathbed, the accuser, Eunice Pringle, confessed that Joseph P. Kennedy had masterminded the frame-up of Pantages because he wanted to take over Pantages' chain of theaters.

In the summer of 1994, I received a call at my Mother's apartment in New York City. On the phone were Ted Wately and Murad Muhammad. Watley had been a contract negotiator for Don King Productions and had developed a reputation of getting fighters to sign, even the *most resistant ones.*   Muhammad had been Razor Ruddock's manager. They related to me that they had been following my efforts during 1992 to clear Mike Tyson's name, and that my allegations were correct about what really had happened. The bottom line was that Don King had bragged to Wately that "Tyson had to be taught a lesson." The fact that Ted Wately thought to call me with this show of support gave me additional courage to carry on this struggle.

On November 1, 1994, I flew into Miami because I got

a call from Camacho. He wanted to speak with me to discuss the future of his boxing career. He already was a three-time champion and felt he could do it again by beating Pernell Whittaker. But he also mentioned he was having "a small problem" with Don King which he needed to talk to me about in person. I met up on South Beach with Elanora Rossellini, a lady client from Italy, for whom I previously had worked as a bodyguard. She happened to be staying in Miami Beach and invited me to dinner at *Senor Frogs* in Coconut Grove.

While we were eating, my beeper went off. It was Camacho's trainer who told me that Camacho had broken camp and was headed to his residence in Clewiston, Florida before making the trip to Miami Beach. He would arrive to meet with me around midnight. I could expect a beep from him at that time. Camacho had been under house arrest in Clewiston as part of the terms of his conditional release after being convicted for assault and battery upon a law-enforcement officer at the Miami International Airport. The officer had been watching Camacho on a surveillance camera and saw him in possession of drugs. Camacho had an additional problem stemming from that case, having been ordered to pay a substantial sum of restitution to the injured officer.

Around 11 p.m. I took Elanora back to the Park Central Hotel on Ocean Drive where we shared a glass of wine in the lobby. At about 11:20 p.m., Camacho paged me. He was close to South Beach and wanted to know my location. Soon, Camacho showed up with two unknown guys at the Park Central, looking wired and paranoid.

"We've gotta' talk," he said.

I told him I had a client with me and couldn't leave her, but he insisted this was "business" and we needed to be alone. After saying my goodbyes to Elanora, I headed with Camacho to The Clevelander Hotel in Camacho's rented Cadillac. He made several calls on the cellular phone that came with the car, but I still didn't have a clue what this was about. At The Clevelander, Camacho went into a rap about the "old days" and started throwing down screwdrivers like they were going out of style. He was acting childish and obnoxious with everybody around us, grabbing every girl in sight by the ass. He was looking very foolish with powder on his nose while he continued to get extremely drunk. I wasn't enjoying this at all.

"I left a bag in the car, Rudy," Camacho finally said. "There's a lot of jewelry there. Go get it. It's on the floor underneath the driver's seat."

Camacho tossed me the keys and turned back to order another screwdriver. Feeling cold and uncomfortable, I exited The Clevelander and walked toward the rented Cadillac. Something clicked inside me. There was a real possibility that my childhood friend was setting me up. I could have turned and gone back inside, but I needed to put this friendship to its final test, whether Hector Camacho was capable of doing me harm. Inside on the floor, just like Camacho had said, there was a small leather clutch. When I returned to the bar, Camacho was out of his chair, dancing and wiggling wildly. I handed him the clutch.

"*You're* my bodyguard. It's important *you* hold on to it," giving me a look which made my skin crawl. "I gotta' go to the can," he said.

Before he entered the men's room, he looked back one more time with that same weird look that scared the shit out of me. Immediately, I knew that I had to ditch that bag. I flung it into a little storage room, then headed for the bathroom to confront Camacho. At that moment a wave of police officers spread across the bar moving directly for me. As they surrounded me, I told them I hadn't done anything wrong. In fact, I told them I was protecting three-time world champion Hector "Macho" Camacho. They said there had been a report that someone fitting my description was impersonating a police officer and robbing pedestrians at gunpoint. They had my full cooperation, I assured them, and made sure they knew I wasn't armed because I wasn't licensed as a bodyguard in Florida. Then I produced identification showing that I was licensed in New York, California, and Nevada. As they frisked me, I noticed that Camacho still hadn't returned from the bathroom. Finally, the police went looking for him.

Among my identification, the police found a badge, bearing the logo of the Police Benevolent Association, given me by one of my friends in the Florida Highway Patrol. This was a problem for the seargant who didn't like the fact I carried a "Florida badge" while not being licensed in Florida. He arrested me for "impersonating a police officer," and I was escorted outside. My name was run through the computer which revealed that my record was clean as a whistle.

As I sat in the back of the police cruiser parked in front of The Clevelander Hotel, Camacho came outside and approached. He had a very confident look on his face as he tapped on the passenger window.

"You should never fuck with Don King! Now you're going to jail!"

I didn't understand what was going on and said: "Stop fooling around. Chill out."

Then I noticed Camacho's gaze moving to the front of the car. My identification and other personal items, taken during the frisk, had been spread across the hood of the cruiser. When he didn't see the leather clutch there, he turned back to me with a shocked expression, realizing that his mission had failed. Camacho had given me the punch line before telling me the joke. With that look of shock, Hector "Macho" Camacho vanished. My case eventually was dropped by the Dade State Attorney in exchange for my agreeement not to seek legal action against the City of Miami Beach. As he disappeared into the darkness that night, the friendship spanning several decades between me and Hector "Macho" Camacho died.

There came a point in time when the judge in the rape trial, Patricia J. Gifford, offered Mike Tyson the opportunity for early release from his six-year sentence. After serving two years and two months, Tyson appeared before her for a hearing. Camille Ewald, then 89-years old, testified on his behalf. There also was testimony from others who told the judge that Tyson was studying and improving himself. Tyson told the judge that his fame and fortune had come too easily, "like it all just dropped from the sky." He said he was "sorry" for the "situation" and for "any pain" caused to Desiree Washington and her family. But he *refused* to admit that he had raped her. Judge Gifford noted that Tyson failed his test for a "G.E.D.", a general equivalency high school diploma. She said that anyone with Tyson's "normal intelligence," and "without a learning disability," should be able to pass the G.E.D. if they work at it. She also considered that Tyson's statements about just "being sorry" didn't cut it. With these two things in mind, Judge Gifford denied his motion for early release.

In an article entitled "Tyson's Moral Choice," Ferdie Pacheco wrote that all Tyson had to do to become a free man, and get back into earning millions of dollars, was to agree to be labeled "Mike Tyson, the Rapist." Pacheco said: "The day Mike Tyson had the courage to make his moral decision is the day Tyson won a great victory. He became an admirable man in my eyes. If he never wins another boxing match, he will go down as `Mike Tyson, Champion.'" In the *Boxing Illustrated* article, Pacheco concluded: "I am proud of Mike Tyson. Tyson's choice is an achievement which exceeds anything he has done before. So, let the wise guys laugh in their beers, I lift my glass to `Mike Tyson, The Man.'"

On May 18, 1992, *Sports Illustrated* reported that Bill Cayton sued Don King, alleging that King skimmed millions from Tyson fight purses. Later, in a deposition in that case, Mohammed Khan, Tyson's former accountant, testified that Tyson is down to a few million dollars worth of assets which included some real estate, a few expensive cars, and a $2.8 million annuity. Joseph Maffia, former Don King Productions comptroller, gave an affidavit in which he testified that much of Tyson's money went to King and his family. Maffia swore that his former boss had skimmed millions off Tyson fight purses before Tyson collected his 66.6% share and King his 33.3% promoter's fee. King responded that Maffia's affidavit was filled with lies, fabrications, and half-truths. "I have never improperly taken anything from Mike and every expense was at his direction or approval," King fired back.

The day that the verdict was handed down convicting Mike Tyson of rape, I believed it was the end. All I wanted to do was distance myself from everything that had been going on, erasing it from memory, as I had done with the pocket computer delivered into the hands of John Horne. But six thousand miles far away from home, as I lay on a beach in Rio de Janeiro, I could not put behind me what had happened over the past six years. Mike Tyson had given me the opportunity of a lifetime and made me part of his inner-ring. He had continued to trust and support me over the years no matter how much others tried to destroy our relationship.

Back in my Mother's apartment in New York, my Tyson jackets were hanging in a closet, representing the real tradition behind this world champion heavyweight fighter. I had seen how so many had cared for him over the years, and how he had cared for them before others took over control of every part of his life. And I had witnessed the deceit and betrayal and fraud committed upon him.

There had been so much light in the first few years and so much darkness during the last two. Once I made the drive to The White House to check up on Camille Ewald who by then had turned 90-years old. Before I went there, I stopped by Junior's in Brooklyn to pick up some of her favorite cheesecake. When I arrived that night, I noticed that Camille had lit a number of candles in the dining room. It turned out that she didn't have enough money to pay her electric bill.

I tried to contact Mike Tyson at the Plainfield, Indiana prison, but all of my letters were returned undelivered, stamped "unauthorized mail." When I called the prison to find out why MT couldn't receive my mail, I was informed that I would have to go through attorneys for Don King Productions. I have done some checking on the inventory of the luxury automobiles, recently learning through a source in Beverly Hills that most of the cars have been auctioned off, many below commercial value, with John Horne getting most of the proceeds. What hasn't been sold has been distributed among King family members and associates.

As the Brazilian sun bathed me in its light and warmth, I could not stop thinking about Mike Tyson sitting alone in a cold and dark prison cell. He never should have been put there. Then I knew exactly what I had to do. Mike Tyson never fired me. As far as I was concerned, I still had a job working for him. The story of Mike Tyson's life did not have to end on that cold day in February of 1992 when an Indianapolis jury handed down its verdict. Instead, another story could begin, one filled with truth and light. I had the Wizard computer disc and the copies made with the hand-held Panasonic copier. These things told a story, about the fraud, deceit, and betrayal committed upon Mike Tyson.

And I continue to believe to this day that I still work for Mike Tyson. *He never fired me.* I haven't been paid for more than three years, since that night I saw him for the last time, getting together his valuables with him at The Big House in Southington, Ohio. But it doesn't matter. I wasn't at MT's side, to watch over him and ensure his *safe passage*, during those early morning hours of July 19, 1991 in Indianapolis. There were forces of darkness which made sure I couldn't be there. I wasn't there for MT that *one night* which forever changed his life. Nothing can be done about that now. But what can be done is that Mike Tyson make a choice for *personal* freedom after being released from prison and regaining his *official* freedom.

In this world, there are not many times where great tragedy can be prevented, where events still are playing out, where history still is being written. Yet, this happens to be one of them. The author, James Baldwin, said: "Freedom is not something that anybody can be given. Freedom is some-

thing people take, and people are as free as they want to be."
The American abolitionist, Frederick Douglas, said: "He who
would be free must strike the first blow."   If MT goes back to
Don King, John Horne, and Rory Holloway, then this will show
that he simply has traded one form of custody for another.
And if this happens, Mike Tyson will never be a free man.

My job always has had one bottom line, *"safe passage
for Mike Tyson."*   But, God willing, after leaving that Indiana
prison cell where he was locked away unjustly for more than
three years, I pray that the *passages* in this story, at least in
some small way, will *safely* guide and protect Mike Tyson for
the rest of his life.

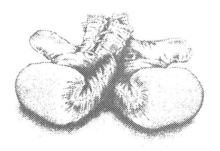

Rudy visiting in Puerto Rico.

Rudy at age 10 in early Akido Martial Arts Training, in Spanish Harlem, New York.

Rudy Gonzalez in some of his Team Tyson Gear.

Choice selections from Tysons fleet of Luxury and Exotic Automobiles.

Underground garage in Atlantic City, N.J. housing some of Tysons east coast cars.

C

Tyson bought them, Rudy drove them and took care of them. Tyson owned one of the most outrageous and expensive exotic car collections.

One of Tyson's Ferrari Testarossas -
It's custom ostrich skin interior along with a
5000 watt Nakamichi sound system made it
a thoroughbred in his stable of Ferrari's.

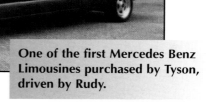

One of the first Mercedes Benz
Limousines purchased by Tyson,
driven by Rudy.

PAYMENT OPTION:	☑ CHECK/MONEY ORDER $40.15	☐ MASTERCARD $41.19	☐ VISA	CHARGE ACCOUNT #		CARD EXP.

493XQRAT2WK

TYSON*MICHAEL
8083 CHUB RD
WINDSOR   OH   44099

PLATE CAT. PASSENGER   PLATE NO. 493XQR   EPA NO

PLATE TYPE   TITLE NO. 040332556   OLD APP. XV73102

VEH. TYPE 2S   YEAR 89   MAKE PORS   WGT.

VIN WPOEB0917KS173064   PURCHASE DATE 10/23/90

REG. WILL EXPIRE 06/30/91   RENEWAL WILL EXPIRE 06/30/92

TAX DIST. 0491   DISTRICT NAME WINDSOR

COUNTY ASHTABULA   SSN OR TAX I.D. NUMBER 089569372

PROOF OF FINANCIAL RESPONSIBILITY

I affirm that I will not operate or permit the operation of a motor vehicle in this state unless proof of financial responsibility is maintained with respect to that vehicle or in the case of a driver who is not the owner, with respect to his operation of that vehicle (O.R.C. Secs. 4503.20 and 4509.101). Requirements of the law and penalty for violation are stated on the back of this form.
I also affirm that my license plate registration is not under suspension or revocation under Ohio Financial Responsibility Law, the vehicle is lawfully entitled to be registered for the above plate category, any required registration or transfer fees have been paid if I operated the vehicle upon public roads or highways prior to the date of this application, and the vehicle will not be used for Farm or Commercial purposes.

SIGNATURE OF OWNER   X   JOINT OWNER SIGNATURE   5/20/91 DATE   BMV-4604

WARNING: Applicant giving false information is subject to prosecution O.R.C. Section 2921.13. Application must be signed by the owner as named on certificate of title.

T2WK A 493XQR 004015 004119 063091 063092 2S89PORS RNWL 2

and the vehicle will not be used for Farm or Commercial purposes.

SIGNATURE OF OWNER   X   JOINT OWNER SIGNATURE   5/21/91 DATE   BMV-460

WARNING: Applicant giving false information is subject to prosecution O.R.C. Section 2921.13. Application must be signed by the owner as named on certificate of title.

T2OF A 1A5V7W 003515 003607 063091 063092 4S84ASTO RNWL

I also affirm that my license plate registration is not under suspension or revocation under Ohio Financial Responsibility Law, the vehicle is lawfully entitled to be registered for the above plate category, any required registration or transfer fees have been paid if I operated the vehicle upon public roads or highways prior to the date of this application, and the vehicle will not be used for Farm or Commercial purposes.

SIGNATURE OF OWNER   X   JOINT OWNER SIGNATURE   5/20/91 DATE   BMV-4604

WARNING: Applicant giving false information is subject to prosecution O.R.C. Section 2921.13. Application must be signed by the owner as named on certificate of title.

T2WL A 740XAJ 004015 004119 063091 063092 2S90MERC RNWL

PROOF OF FINANCIAL RESPONSIBILITY

I affirm that I will not operate or permit the operation of a motor vehicle, with respect to his operation of that vehicle (O.R.C. Secs. 4503.20 and 4509.101. Requirements of the law and penalty for violation are case of a driver who is not the owner, with respect to his operation of that vehicle (O.R.C. Secs. 4503.20 and 4509.101. Requirements of the law and penalty for violation are stated on the back of this form.
I also affirm that my license plate registration is not under suspension or revocation under Ohio Financial Responsibility Law, the vehicle is lawfully entitled to be registered for the above plate category, any required registration or transfer fees have been paid if I operated the vehicle upon public roads or highways prior to the date of this application, and the vehicle will not be used for Farm or Commercial purposes.

089569372

SIGNATURE OF OWNER   X   JOINT OWNER SIGNATURE   5/21/91 DATE   BMV-4604

WARNING: Applicant giving false information is subject to prosecution O.R.C. Section 2921.13. Application must be signed by the owner as named on certificate of title.

T2OF A 183VZW 003515 003607 063091 063092 4S85ROLS RNWL 2

Compare Mike Tyson's actual signature below, to the registration forms signed above

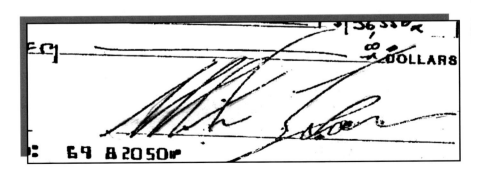

F

TEAM TYSON ~ top row: John Horne, Anthony Pitts, Rudy Gonzalez, Gladys Rosa, Don King. bottom row: Mike Tyson and Rory Holloway.

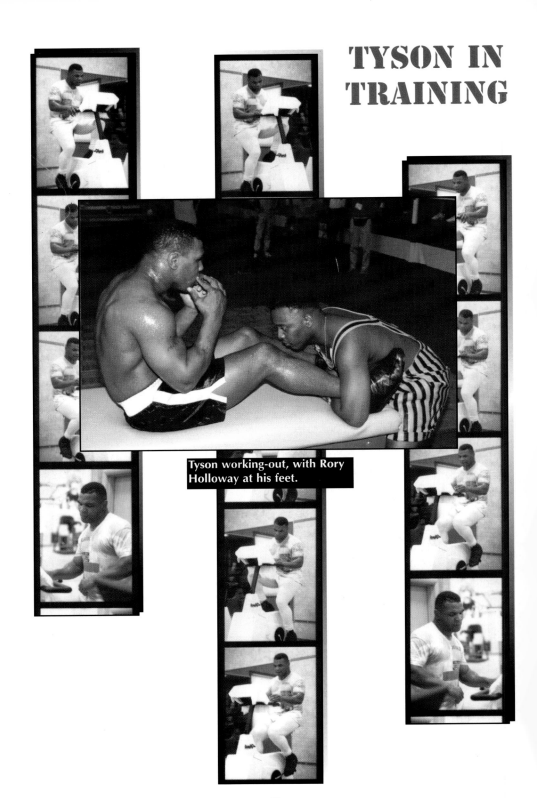

TYSON IN TRAINING

Tyson working-out, with Rory Holloway at his feet.

Rory Holloway and John Horne

Tyson, asleep at a press conference.

Champ sized ~ 10kt. diamond ring

Mike & his female fans.

J

Mike Tyson in Luxury Hotel Suite in Europe.

Tyson in Jeff Hamilton leather.

Scale model of Genesis Coach
planned to be built for Tyson's escape from King.

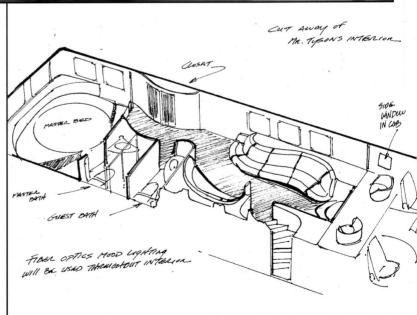

Sketch of interior ~ 2 bedroom luxury
accommodations including gold fixtures.

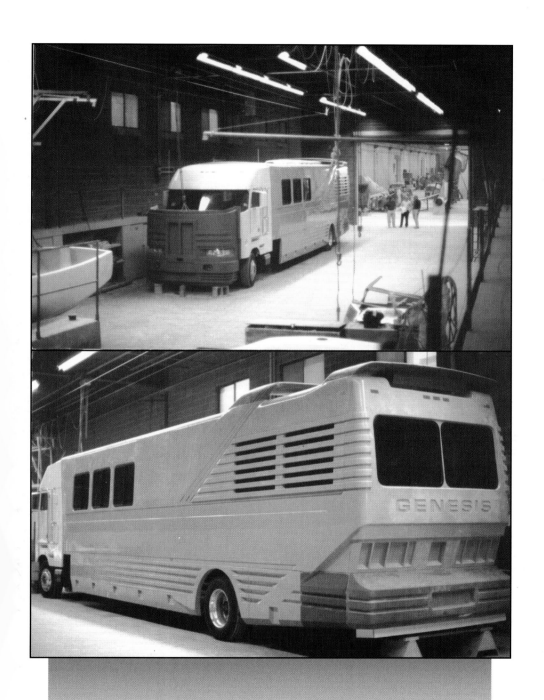

The Genesis Coach under construction in New York.

The Genesis Coach on the road in Las Vegas.

Sample of Rudy's payroll checks from Mike Tyson.

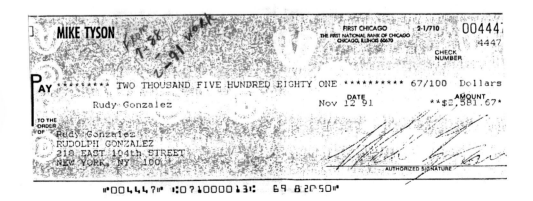

MIKE TYSON   255

LAST CHECK BY ME
ISSUED TO RUDY.   7/23 1991   2-1/
Mildred 9/7/91
PAY TO THE
ORDER OF RUDOLPH GONZALEZ $ 3750.00

THREE THOUSAND SEVEN HUNDRED FIFTY   00 DOLLA

FIRST CHICAGO
The First National Bank of Chicago
Chicago, Illinois 60670

FOR WAGER :- 6/28 - 7/16/91

⑈00255⑈ ⑈071000013⑈ 69 82050⑈

MIKE TYSON   451
TRAINING ACCOUNT

NOVEMBER 16, 19 90   56-70/412

PAY TO THE
ORDER OF RUDY GONZALEZ $ 1,500.00

ONE THOUSAND FIVE HUNDRED AND NO/100   DOLLARS
06-89-02

Society BANK of Eastern Ohio   ORWELL OHIO 44076

FOR 2 WEEKS W/C 11/9 & 11/16

⑈000451⑈ ⑈041200704⑈45⑈876 9464⑈

MIKE TYSON   FIRST CHICAGO   2-1/710   004447
                              THE FIRST NATIONAL BANK OF CHICAGO
                              CHICAGO, ILLINOIS 60670   4447
                                                    CHECK
                                                    NUMBER

PAY ******** TWO THOUSAND FIVE HUNDRED EIGHTY ONE ********* 67/100 Dollars

         Rudy Gonzalez   Nov 12 91   **$2,581.67*
                                    DATE   AMOUNT

TO THE
ORDER
OF Rudy Gonzalez
    RUDOLPH GONZALEZ
    218 EAST 104th STREET
    NEW YORK, NY 100   AUTHORIZED SIGNATURE

⑈004447⑈ ⑈071000013⑈ 69 82050⑈

Contract for purchase of Lamborghini

P

Controversial Exotic
This 1991 Lamborghini Diablo was purchased by Mike Tyson, cost $ 442,189.45 ~ The first and only car ever registered in Mike Tyson's name.

The KING of Propaganda ~ Don King

BROWN

HARRIS

STEVENS

ESTABLISHED 1873

May 2, 1991

Dear Mr Gonzalez

Enclosed please find a floor plan on penthouse A at
161 West 61st. (the Alfred condominium).

It is truly a spectacular apartment. I would be
pleased to show you the property. If you would like
further information, please call me at 212-906-9291.

I look forward to hearing from you soon —

Very truly yours

████████████

655 MADISON AVENUE, NEW YORK, N.Y. 10021 ◆ 212 593-8300

**Letter written to Rudy by real estate agent who
witnessed altercation between Mike Tyson and Don King.**

PHONE WALKER 5-4881

JOHN JOVINO CO.
DISTRIBUTORS OF FIREARMS
Police Equipment
5 CENTRE MARKET PLACE
NEW YORK 13, N. Y.

R 15237

DATE 5/2/19 91

BOUGHT FROM

SOLD TO _DON KING PRODUCTIONS_
32 EAST 69TH STREET
New York, N.Y. 1002

OCC	AGE	HEIGHT	WEIGHT	TIME	PERMIT NO.		SHIELD NO.	

QUANTITY	DESCRIPTION	PRICE		TOTAL	
1	POINT BLANK MOD 15 SIDE PANEL WHITE 46R (TAKEN)			850	00
1	POINT BLANK MOD 15 SIDE PANEL WHITE 46R (BACK ORDER) TO BE SHIPPED				
	Paid in full ck# 001473				

Receipt for Bullet-Proof vest purchased by King on the day
Tyson confronted King regarding financial irregularities
discovered by Tyson and Rudy.

T

The Ferrari Koening that Tyson purchased -and wrecked, frequently.

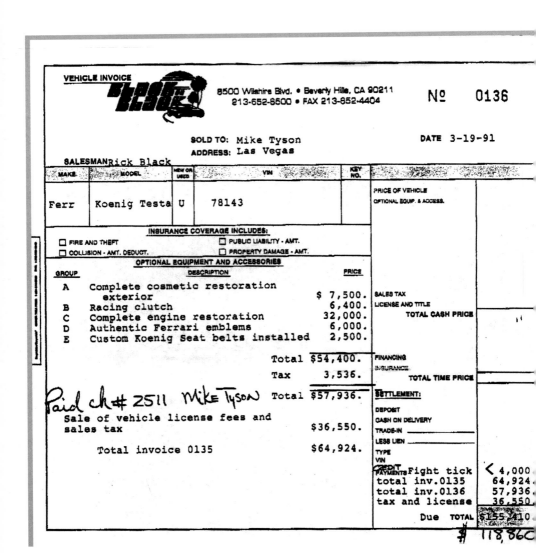

8500 Wilshire Blvd. • Beverly Hills, CA 90211
213-652-8500 • FAX 213-652-4404

Nº   0136

SOLD TO: Mike Tyson
ADDRESS: Las Vegas

DATE 3-19-91

SALESMAN Rick Black

MAKE	MODEL	NEW OR USED	VIN	KEY NO.		PRICE OF VEHICLE
Ferr	Koenig Testa	U	78143			OPTIONAL EQUIP. & ACCESS.

INSURANCE COVERAGE INCLUDES:

☐ FIRE AND THEFT   ☐ PUBLIC LIABILITY - AMT.
☐ COLLISION - AMT. DEDUCT.   ☐ PROPERTY DAMAGE - AMT.

OPTIONAL EQUIPMENT AND ACCESSORIES

GROUP	DESCRIPTION	PRICE
A	Complete cosmetic restoration exterior	$ 7,500.
B	Racing clutch	6,400.
C	Complete engine restoration	32,000.
D	Authentic Ferrari emblems	6,000.
E	Custom Koenig Seat belts installed	2,500.
	Total	$54,400.
	Tax	3,536.
	Total	$57,936.

SALES TAX
LICENSE AND TITLE
   TOTAL CASH PRICE

FINANCING
INSURANCE
   TOTAL TIME PRICE

SETTLEMENT:
DEPOSIT
CASH ON DELIVERY
TRADE-IN _____
LESS LIEN _____
TYPE
VIN
CREDIT

Paid ck # 2511 Mike Tyson

Sale of vehicle license fees and
sales tax $36,550.

   Total invoice 0135 $64,924.

PAYMENTS Fight tick < 4,000.
total inv.0135   64,924.
total inv.0136   57,936.
tax and license   36,550.

Due   TOTAL $155,410.

118,860

What Tyson pays for automobile repairs!

Mr. Don King
32 East 69th Street
New York, New York 10021

Dec.,11,90

Re: Mike Tyson Ferrari purchase agreement

Dear Mr.King,

Kindly be advised of confirmation to our conversation
today december 11th,1990 of Mr.Tyson's purchase of a
1988 Ferrari Testarosa spyder convertible Koenig Special
with Vin# 2FFAA17B000078143. It is hereby agreed:

  (1) Mr.Tyson is taking delivery of the vehicle today under
     a borrowed car agreement pursuant to your verbal
     authorization of payment via wire transfer to our
     account on December 12th,1990 of $430,000.00 as well
     as providing insurance coverage for the vehicle.

  (2) The vehicle must be returned to Black Imports on or
     before December 15,1990 for DOT/EPA certification
     and transport to Mr.Tyson's home in Las Vegas,
     Nevada for title and license.

  (3) Four ringside seats to Mike Tyson fight with Evander
     Hollyfield.

Please have your office confirm the wire transfer with
a Federal Reserve number for our tracking purpose. You will
find attached our Bank wire information. We have attached
documents for your records of the purchase agreement and
vehicle specifications.

Please sign below where indicated and return via fax.

                        Sincerely,

                        Rick Black, President

Accepted and agreed
Don King

Exh A

Some of Rudy's hundreds of tickets showing his travel with Tyson.

More Airline Tickets...

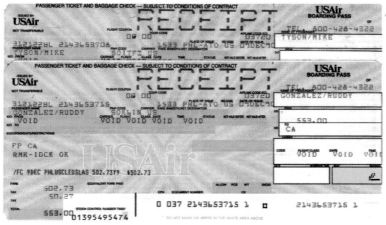

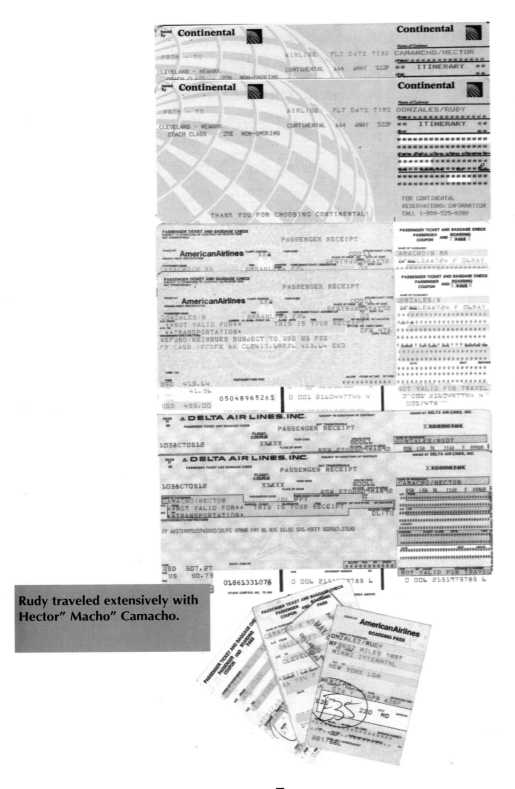

Rudy traveled extensively with Hector" Macho" Camacho.

Z

Julio " Cesar" Chavez, prior to his troubles with Don King.

World Famous Leather Designer Jeff Hamilton with Mike.

IRON MIKE TYSON

DD

MIKE TYSON PRODUCTIONS, INC

C/O DON KING PRODUCTIONS, INC
32 EAST 69th STREET
NEW YORK, NEW YORK 10021
(212) 794-2900

<u>Via Certified Mail</u>

August 17, 1992

Mr. Rudolph Gonzalez
218 East 104th Street
Apartment 2H
New York, New York 10029

Dear Rudy:

This is to confirm my previous verbal requests to you to return all
of Mike Tyson's property and personal possessions that you have in
your possession. I was informed that you have the following items:

    Bullet proof vests
    Beepers
    Jewelry
    Clothing
    Luggage
    Wizard computer and printer
    Documents for cars:- bills of sale and titles
    Cameras
    Album with picture of cars

You were terminated over six months ago. I request you immediately
drop off these items and any others that you have for Mr. Tyson at
my office at 32 East 69th Street, NY, NY 10021 or let me know where
and when I can have them picked up. I would appreciate if we could
handle this matter by ourselves without having to get Mike's
attorneys involved.

Thank you for your prompt attention to this matter. I can be
reached by telephone at 212-794-2900 ext. 3012 or at the above
address.

Yours sincerely,

Mohamed Khan

Mohamed Khan
Accountant

**Copy of letter written to Rudy by Don Kings'
Accountant. Rudy was NEVER terminated by *his*
employer ~ Mike Tyson.**

cc: Mike Tyson
     Don King
     John Horne
     Rory Holloway

EE

INNER RING™ GEAR

TO ORDER YOUR OFFICIAL

INNER RING™
T-SHIRT, HOODED SWEATSHIRT
OR BASEBALL CAP
CALL 1-800-619-2BOX (2269)

VISA • MC • AMEX

HOODED SWEATSHIRTS	**$25.95**
T-SHIRTS	**$19.95**
BASEBALL CAPS	**$14.95**
THE INNER RING (BOOK)	**$19.95**

ADD 4.95 S&H (PER ITEM) - ALLOW 2-3 WEEKS FOR DELIVERY

OR SEND PERSONAL CHECK OR MONEY ORDER TO
THE OLIVER PUBLISHING GROUP
C/O WHITEHURST & CLARK
100 NEW FIELD AVENUE
EDISON, NEW JERSEY 08837